the kitchen shrink

How the food we eat reveals who we are - and how we love

Dr Andrea Oskis

BLOOMSBURY PUBLISHING
LONDON · OXFORD · NEW YORK · NEW DELHI · SYDNEY

BLOOMSBURY PUBLISHING
Bloomsbury Publishing Plc
50 Bedford Square, London, WC1B 3DP, UK
29 Earlsfort Terrace, Dublin 2, Ireland

BLOOMSBURY, BLOOMSBURY PUBLISHING and the Diana logo
are trademarks of Bloomsbury Publishing Plc

First published in Great Britain 2025

A catalogue record for this book is available from the British Library

ISBN: HB: 978-1-5266-7871-3; TPB: 978-1-5266-7974-1; EBOOK: 978-1-5266-7972-7;
EPDF: 978-1-5266-7977-2

2 4 6 8 10 9 7 5 3 1

Typeset by Newgen KnowledgeWorks Pvt. Ltd., Chennai, India
Printed and bound in Great Britain by CPI Group (UK) Ltd, Croydon CR0 4YY

To find out more about our authors and books visit www.bloomsbury.com
and sign up for our newsletters

For Delia

How complicated things get when food
and love become hopelessly tangled.
Nora Ephron, *Heartburn* (1983)

This book is for anyone who has ever wondered why.

CONTENTS

CONTENTS

TO START

I am sitting in my favourite chair in my clinic, listening to a new patient. Like most patients, she has come to therapy because of a problem in love. She says her husband doesn't love her anymore, and she is wondering why their relationship has gone wrong.

I ask her a question, and the answer she gives me feels like opening the fridge door and seeing everything inside become illuminated. It is a light-bulb moment, you might say, and one that defines my whole career from then on. This is the question I ask: 'When did you know he didn't love you anymore?'

And this is what she says: 'It wasn't when we stopped having sex. No, it was when he stopped eating dinner with me.'

That was the moment I discovered there is no better way to get inside people's lives than through what they eat. The stories that tell me the most about a person are not clichéd ones about loving their mother, or hating their father, or being rivals with their siblings. The most revealing stories are the ones about food.

For the past twenty years, my work has been based around attachment theory, the best known, most significant and longest-established explanation of love and relationships. No single theory has been researched more in psychology during the last three decades. This is because it asks some 'big' questions: how we live, love, cope, change, grow and let go. The answers to all of these, according to attachment theory, have one key ingredient: our nearest and dearest. We all make emotional bonds with particular people, this is what makes us human. And this is what also makes you, *you*. Attachment theory can be thought of as being a bit like a recipe that tells you how and why your experiences of close relationships make you the person you are. And the more familiar you are with the recipe, the better – which is why I wanted to write this book. Attachment theory and research are at the heart of what I do every day as a psychotherapist and as an academic.

As far as theories go, attachment theory is not very old. It was created in the 1950s, which makes it younger than my first attachment figure – my mother. She is still one of the people I can count on when things go wrong, in life and in the kitchen. My family is Greek Cypriot, so food is, and has always been, a big part of life. Perhaps it's no wonder that in recent years, I've been focusing on the role food plays in relationships.

Everyone's attachment story starts once upon a table. We come into this world as a tiny, helpless human being, and when we get hungry, lo and behold, food and the person who takes care of us turn up together. There is something very special on the menu: an opportunity for a relationship. The food of love is, well, food. When we are fed, we get to feel safe, secure, soothed and loved: *this* is attachment. But attachments are not just for babies; we have these unique relationship bonds throughout life. John Bowlby, a British psychiatrist and psychoanalyst, and one of the founders of attachment theory, famously said that attachment is a human behaviour 'from the cradle to the grave'. And along the way, it shows up at the table and in the kitchen more than you might think.

When I teach attachment theory at university, I don't start with Bowlby, or any other psychologist for that matter. I arrive for the first lecture of term armed with my dog-eared copies of M. F. K. Fisher's *The Gastronomical Me*, Margaret Visser's *Much Depends On Dinner* and Nigella Lawson's *How to Eat*. I hold up the books and tell the students that food writing has a lot to say about attachment. Some look curious, others look at me as though I'm one sandwich short of a picnic. I then start my presentation by showing them a slide with the famous food saying by Brillat-Savarin, and I ask them to fill in the gap: 'Tell me what you eat and I will tell you who you ____'

The students shout the word 'Are!' into the lecture theatre, which is correct.

I say: 'But what if you replace that word with "love"?'

Then things get interesting because, as M. F. K. Fisher puts it, food and love and security are 'mixed and mingled and entwined'.

So, tell me, what do you eat that makes you feel safe and soothed, like your loved one is holding your hand? Who gives you the confidence to get out of your comfort food zone and explore the world around you? What happens to your appetite when you are alone – is it food or relationships that really feed you? Have you ever, as Nigella suggests you should, eaten a whole chocolate fudge cake when your heart was broken? Your story of attachment is written on your plate.

This is not your typical food book. We've all read about crisp green salads, light-as-air soufflés and meltingly tender lamb shanks. In this book, the food is inviting for different reasons. The saying goes that the nearer the bone, the sweeter the meat. The food in these stories takes us close to the bone, to what truly matters most: our intimate attachments to other human beings. Here is a taste of what's to come. We will discover the real reason why comfort food comforts, why dessert isn't a good idea when you're stressed, and how grief can be sunny side up with the help of a few eggs. We'll see why family-style food sharing doesn't always mean happy families, and what makes children feel obliged to eat their beans and greens. I will show you how television cooks make great attachment figures. I will tell you why you should *never* give a bottle of hot sauce to someone who has been rejected. Through these stories, I want to help you to love and be loved better by changing your understanding of two of the things we need for life, from the cradle to the grave: relationships and food. Be prepared to never look at your plate – or Nigella or Delia – in the same way again.

Part I
ATTACHMENT

Cupboard Love

*Why is food an important ingredient
in your first relationship?*

'It wasn't Mum Food,' my patient, Rose, said to me.

'Mum Food?' I said, a little confused, hoping Rose would enlighten me. Perhaps she was talking about yet another food fad that had passed me by, like the cruffin or the cronut (I haven't tried either). I'm not very on trend food-wise, or really very fashionable in other ways. I have, it seems, turned into one of those therapists who wear cardigans. I sat back in my chair, cosy in my chunky knit, and listened as Rose continued.

'Yes, you know, Mum Food: food that gives you that feeling of *mmmm* or *ahhh*, like you're safe and sound,' Rose looked at me. It felt like she was searching for acknowledgement in my eyes.

The penny dropped. There was nothing trendy about what Rose was describing. In fact, she was talking about something that is guaranteed never to go out of fashion: our universal human need for security. What we really mean when we talk about psychological security is to have someone be there for us in a way that makes us feel safe and loved. This was how Rose felt about her mother and, most specifically, her Mum Food.

'There was no "other" in "mother" with my mum. She was born to be a mum,' Rose said, as she went on to tell me about her mother's complete and utter devotion to her when she was a child. Rose's mother loved all aspects of caring for her daughter, especially cooking for her. Every week she would make Rose's favourite dish: apple pie.

My curiosity was piqued. I love a pie. Pies have actually been pretty significant in my academic life. We performed *Boston Marriage* by David Mamet for A-Level drama, and I played one of the lead characters, Claire. The most magnificent line of the play was mine: 'We must have a pie. Stress cannot exist in the presence of a pie.' It got a lot of laughs from the audience. More recently, at the university where I lecture, on open days we stage a moment during the welcome speech where an audience member who, unbeknown to the prospective students, is really a member of staff, runs up onto the stage and pies our Head of Department. That also gets a lot of laughs each year, but really it's to demonstrate the psychology of eyewitness testimony.

Rose continued our conversation with details of her mother's apple pie. Rose was an English teacher, so she loved language and a good description you could sink your teeth into. I heard all the usual adjectives: golden, buttery, crumbly, cinnamon-y, but her northern Welsh accent had a singsong quality to it that made the whole thing dreamy. It was 7.30 a.m. but I could have eaten this pie right there and then. The description was so evocative that for a minute I floated away on it. Then Rose said a word that brought me down off my cloud and back to earth: 'Hobnob'.

My confusion returned.

Then came the big reveal: there was no pastry. Rose's mother would crush up Hobnob biscuits, mix them with butter and press the mixture on top of the apple filling. According to food historian Janet Clarkson, this breaks the first law of pies: 'No pastry, no pie'. This apple pie, with its pretend pastry, wasn't really a pie. But that didn't matter to Rose and her mother, because 'pie' was what they called it. To paraphrase Shakespeare, a pie by any other name would not taste as sweet. It was this pie that was Rose's Mum Food.

'Don't they say you need cold hands to make pastry? Mum's were far too warm. That pie was like being hugged in her arms,' Rose glowed as she smiled. I found myself feeling comfortable and warm – and this time it wasn't just my cardigan. Stress did not exist in the presence of Rose's mum's pie. I think we were both soothed by it. In an almost Proustian way, I was experiencing what it felt like to be in the presence of Rose's mother. Or rather, to be attached to her.

Rose's mother's apple pie may have broken the first law of pies, but many acts of attachment were contained within it. This pie was full of special 'mum touches' that showed Rose she was seen and understood. It was easy to make, so Rose could join in, and there was nothing Rose loved more than baking. It was fun: Rose learned that rolling pins were for joyfully bashing biscuits, not for rolling out pastry seriously and accurately. There was a lovely ritual and regularity that enveloped the whole thing: Rose knew exactly what to expect ('Friday is Pieday!'). Rose's mother took her daughter's apple needs seriously, and made a playful Goldilocks game out of it: green Granny Smiths were too bitter and Red Delicious were too scary because of the association with the poisonous apple in *Snow White*. So the pie was always made with sunny sweet Golden Delicious apples, which were 'just right'. And of course, the 'pastry' was made with Rose's favourite biscuits. This pie was deep-filled with Rose's feelings about her relationship with her mother.

Rose's feelings about her father, however, were quite different. There was stress and tension in the relationship, and there always had been. No pie could lessen it. Rose's parents had divorced when she was seven years old. They shared custody, but they didn't share much else when it came to parenting. Rose's mother 'filled the house with love'; she was warm and sensitive and always there. As Rose said, 'She loved me to the moon and back.' Rose's father was hot-headed and defensive and he wasn't very present after the divorce, but he 'always put food on the table'. It was true: there was food on the table every night when Rose was there, and the cupboards, fridge and freezer were full. But it wasn't Mum Food.

Rose's father worked long hours, so when Rose was there he paid for wraparound care, and she went to breakfast and after-school clubs. Rose was often the last child to be picked up; she never knew when her father would turn up at the school gate. On the way home, they would usually pick up a takeaway for dinner, despite the bursting kitchen cupboards.

'He had culinary connections,' said Rose. 'He was best friends with Ronald McDonald, the KFC Colonel and the Burger King. If he could, he would have lived in a Pizza Hut – that was his favourite. We had pizza every Friday when I was at his.' Rose's smile turned into a little laugh, and this time her eyes darted upwards. 'He was such a dreadful cook he could burn a takeaway.'

When Rose's father did cook, his go-to dishes were cauliflower cheese, macaroni cheese or a cheese toastie.

'I don't even like cheese!' Rose said to me, her cheeks flaring like her namesake.

There was clearly no care or love or *mmmm* in her father's food; I was almost waiting for Rose to describe it with *arghh*. Those *mmmms* with which Rose had defined Mum Food said a good deal. Psychologists have found that gustatory *mmmms* are a real thing: they are an important part of social interaction between parent and child during mealtimes. For Rose, those *mmmms* had become lifelong *ahhhs* of a soothing and secure attachment to her mother, and they were the sounds she still made in the presence of her mother's apple pie now, as an adult.

There was a bond, of sorts, between Rose and her father. But it wasn't a secure one, in babyhood, childhood and beyond. Something more was needed than just providing food. Rose's father wasn't very on trend, theoretically speaking. In fact, his thinking was pretty old. Around a hundred years ago, 'cupboard love' was the name given to Sigmund Freud's theory that a child becomes attached to their parent because of food, not because of the relationship that came with it. You could say the focus was on the cupboard, figuratively that is, rather than love.

When Rose stayed at her father's house, she didn't feel much love at all. She felt lonely, and she really missed her mother. However, there was something – or someone – who helped her feel better. A woman who was there reliably and consistently, and who knew how to cook.

'It was in the evening. Definitely a school night, around eight when I should have been in bed. I had a TV in my room and I would watch Delia Smith's *Summer Collection*,' said Rose, as the glow returned to her face. 'When the theme tune came on, I just felt calm. I thought she was wonderful, and her recipes too. I loved her huge lazy Susan kitchen table!'

I smiled. I knew exactly what she was talking about. My mother used to record the show every week for me when I was growing up.

'There was this one episode where Delia made a strawberry granita,' Rose said. 'Teeny tiny crimson crystals, like

Barbie rubies, piled high in a sundae glass, garnished with a sprig of mint. The next day I asked my dad if we could make it together. He gave me money to buy a Mr Frosty Ice Maker instead.'

Rose went on. 'Then in another episode, Delia made muffins for her husband's cricket match. My dad played cricket too. So I decided to make muffins for him the next time he had a cricket match,' Rose said. 'He didn't notice them in the kitchen when he eventually came home. Probably because he'd drunk too much after the game. At least Delia showed up when she was meant to. Exactly on time, every week, she would be there.'

It seemed that Rose had experienced the 'Delia effect': Delia Smith had the ingredients of a good attachment figure that Rose's father didn't possess.

'Delia always said what she did and did what she said. My dad didn't, ever. He worked a lot, in the city, in finance. Still does. He's a banker. Rhymes with...' As Rose trailed off, I picked up on the invitation she had given me. I might be an uncool, cardigan-wearing therapist, but I can pun with the rest of them. So I did.

'It feels to me like there's a big thorn in there, Rose,' I said. Rose laughed, gently and warmly. It was a moment of connection between us. I had shown Rose that I could see the anger she had stored up about her father's cupboard love. And in her own way, she had felt safe enough to let me in and show this to me. Rose didn't take up my invitation to explore her thorny comment in our session that day.

I sensed that she wanted to keep things emotionally 'just right' for now.

Rose wasn't the only person who had little love for cupboard love. The father of attachment theory, John Bowlby, did too. For Bowlby, food was a sore subject. When he presented his first major article on attachment, he was booed by Freud's followers because his ideas about feeding were different from cupboard love and other popular psychoanalytic theories. Bowlby took the rejection deeply personally, and it became a defining moment for him professionally. Afterwards, and for the rest of his career, Bowlby expressed distaste towards anyone who said food was important for attachment.

Because of this, Bowlby got into a food fight (academically, not literally) with the mother of attachment theory, Mary Ainsworth. Her research showed that when children were hungry for food, they were also hungry for attachment. In her studies of mothers and babies, feeding was the first and foremost way to provide care, comfort and closeness. She saw that a lot of feelings were stirred up during feeding and weaning; it was powerful and complex for both parent and child. And it was important that this was all handled with care, because it had long-term consequences. Ainsworth therefore believed that Bowlby should big-up food in his trilogy of books, *Attachment, Separation* and *Loss*. She wrote him a letter in 1967 in which her exact words were: 'I do think that feeding can become entangled with the development of attachment, and something more is needed here.' But Bowlby was still busy licking his wounds, and he chose to ignore Ainsworth's concerns. The door firmly closed on food, and it continued to be for a long time in attachment theory and research.

The most powerful finding in Ainsworth's research was that feeding predicted how secure the child's later attachments were with others. Fast-forward twenty-five years, and this was what had brought Rose to see me. Rose was struggling in her attachment to her partner, Florian. Rose had said that she and Florian weren't 'emulsifying as a couple' (what a description) and that they fought 'like cat and dog the whole time they were together'. They were caught in a push-pull dynamic and repelling each other's needs: Rose was dependent, but Florian was distant, and not dependable. Rose was right – they were just like an unstable emulsion, always on the verge of separating unless shaken up by an argument. What they argued about most was Florian 'not being there'. Rose never knew when to expect him home; Florian would often go out with colleagues for 'long, boozy lunches' and come back late in the evening. Rose cooked dinner for both of them most nights, but she ended up eating on her own. When Florian provided food, it wasn't Mum Food either. It was expensive food at fancy restaurants. Rose hated going to these places to eat, but Florian always insisted. Last week, she had jokingly said that she didn't want to go to the 'The Poison Ivy' for dinner.

'All hell broke loose when I said that. He was shouting, "Look how much I love you. I take you to all the best restaurants to eat," and I was screaming back "It doesn't feel like love!" As Rose said this, she looked at me with wide eyes like a lost deer.

The thing is, Rose was lost – in the past. As some therapists say, if it's hysterical then it's historical – and I say it's also relational. Rose's attachment past was being replayed in the present, and it was showing us that something else wasn't emulsifying. Her relationships with men and women were split. On one side, there were Rose's father and Florian just providing food, and on the other, Rose's mother and Delia Smith offering food and something more: love. Rose had a style in her attachments, with rose-tinted glasses on for women and off for men. Maybe I was on the same side as Rose's mother and Delia Smith: I was also a woman who was there for her every week. Untangling all of this was the core of mine and Rose's work in therapy, and that day our conversation about Mum Food had been the starter for that.

In the beginning, food is served with an opportunity for love and attachment. It is the best opportunity for connection that a parent and child can have. At the start of the story that became attachment theory, Ainsworth agreed with Bowlby that the need for food wasn't the cause of attachment, like cupboard love suggested. But she saw something special happen during feeding that she didn't see in any other interaction. I think Ainsworth would have got along well with the food writer Margaret Visser, who wisely pointed out, food is 'never just something to eat'.

Food opens the door to so many things that are important for attachment. To the child, feeder, protector, playmate, comforter and carer are all the same person. These were all the qualities that Rose had found in her mother, and in that pie. But not in her father, whose food had been dished up without any attachment security.

Food is entangled in our first attachment relationships, and it is when we are fed that we start to consider some big questions about love and our loved one: Does this person turn up? Does this person respond? Does this person give me what I need? Is this all done with care and sensitivity? Through our experiences of getting hungry and being fed, we find answers to these questions, and begin to learn what to expect from others. We start developing our own life-long 'recipe' for relationships. In your early years, you are learning more than just whether your breakfast, lunch or dinner (or a pie) turns up. You are learning whether love turns up.

* * *

Apple Pie

This is a mixing and mingling of both Rose's and my mother's apple pies (it's the only homemade dessert she makes, so that makes it special). A lot of Greek desserts are given the name *pita*, which means 'pie'. Greeks would call this a *milopita*, even though traditionally a *milopita* is an apple cake; they don't seem to care about the laws of pies either. But I do. So, in this law-abiding pie there is pastry, in the form of filo. And the ingredients are pretty much things the cupboard (and the fridge) loves.

Serves 4

4 Golden Delicious apples
1 tablespoon lemon juice
2 tablespoons caster sugar
1 teaspoon cornflour
1 teaspoon ground cinnamon
¼ teaspoon ground allspice
4–6 sheets filo pastry
2 tablespoons melted butter
1 tablespoon icing sugar

Grease an ovenproof rectangular dish (approximately 22 x 17 x 6cm) with a little butter or oil. Preheat the oven to 180°C/160°C fan/gas mark 4.

Peel, core and slice the apples as thinly as you can. Put the apples in the dish and sprinkle over the lemon juice. Stir together the caster sugar, cornflour, cinnamon and allspice in a small bowl and scatter over the lemony apples. Mix to make sure everything is combined.

Brush one of the filo sheets with melted butter. Tear the sheet into quarters using your hands, or cut it with a knife. Scrunch up each piece loosely and place it on top of the apples. Repeat with the rest of the filo sheets. You may need more or less filo depending on the size of your dish, but what you are aiming for is enough scrunched-up sheets to give you a ratio of half pastry to half fruit, in terms of depth. When you have finished arranging the filo, brush any remaining melted butter over the top of the pie.

Bake in the oven for 35 minutes. When the pie is ready, the pastry will be deeply golden and crisp. If you are using an oven-safe glass dish, you will be able to see the apples bubbling underneath. Allow to cool for 10 minutes, then sift over the icing sugar. Serve with vanilla ice cream.

2

No Man Is an Île Flottante

*What does your comfort food say
about your childhood?*

My own attachment story started on an island. My father is from a largish one in the middle of the Mediterranean: Cyprus. He came to the UK in the 1970s and settled in a little suburb in north London. It was here that he met my other attachment figure, my mother. She also has Greek Cypriot heritage, but the strongest connection she had to the motherland was the fact that her hometown was an area in London officially called Palmers Green, but known as 'Palmers Greek'. My mother and father became attached, got married and lived happily ever after. After they sorted out my father's visa problems, that is.

You could say that food actually saved my parents' marriage. This is because food was the thing that stopped my father from being deported. Many marriages end over food, but my parents' is not one of them.

One day, a few months after they were married, my mother heard a knock at the door at around 9 p.m. It was a man from the Home Office, and he wanted to check to see if my father was there at home with her. Apparently, the way to verify that my parents' marriage was not a marriage of convenience was to pop by at an inconvenient time. The Home Office man came in, my mother made him a cup of tea, and then he said he wanted to ask my mother and father some questions individually, to see if they really knew each other.

The Home Office man asked my parents all sorts of things, but there was a standout question that he greedily wanted not one, not two, but three answers to. He asked each for the other's top three favourite foods.

I mean, it's not exactly *Jeopardy!*, but it is a profound question. Then again, I am biased because this is a food book you're reading right now. This was how they answered:

My mother said my father's favourite foods
were: avgolemoni (chicken soup with eggs,
lemon and rice), *gemista* (stuffed vegetables) and
galaktoboureko (syrup-soaked, custard-filled filo
pastry).
My father said my mother's favourite foods
were: tinned chicken soup, pie and mash, and
treacle tart and custard.

From their responses, I can imagine the man from the Home Office was quite confused about their marriage. But the story ended well. My parents' answers were crossed-checked and they passed with flying colours. They had the green light to get on with being married, and my mother fully embraced her new-found wifeliness and got on with learning how to cook. Because my mother, as you'll have noticed from my father's answers, is not your typical Greek mama when it comes to food. Neither was her mama. Lovingly prepared, home-cooked food wasn't a big thing in my mother's upbringing. There is no story about how she stood at the kitchen counter as a child next to her mother, watching and helping her cook. I didn't see my maternal grandmother much at all during my childhood. The only kitchen-relevant memory I have about my maternal grand-mother is that she often gave my mother knives as birthday and Christmas gifts. There is certainly some symbolism there, but I was just a child and not a therapist at that point.

Despite learning how to cook, there was no way my mother was giving up her first love – convenience foods – when she married my father. She adored anything tinned or canned or vacuumed-packed, and would always opt for a handy gadget if she had to prep things from scratch. My mother didn't enjoy home-cooked food that much because she didn't find much comfort in it. But we did. By the time my brother and I were born, she'd certainly perfected my father's favourite dinner dishes. She still loves using her 'vegetable drill' to make *gemista*, and her *avgolemoni* is so good. The soup contains eggs, and as part of the tempering process you have to do a lot of whisking, which my mother has a real knack for (I once tried to whisk eggs like my mother and ended up quite knackered from it). The secret to her recipe is pudding rice, which makes the soup really creamy. I think it's one of her best dishes, but my mother still prefers tinned chicken soup.

One day, chicken soup came into the session with my patient Brontë—both the homemade and the tinned variety. That day, Brontë had news to tell me: she said it was 'over' with her boyfriend, Eliot, whom she had been with for just over a year. In therapy, Brontë had said plenty about what was wrong in the relationship – or really, what Eliot was doing wrong in the relationship – from the moment she came to see me a few months prior. In fact, she spoke a lot about Eliot in general. I had got to know him quite well; in some ways, perhaps better than Brontë. I knew that Eliot was a chef and that he'd worked in some really well-known restaurants all around the world. He enjoyed exploring new cuisines, discovering new ingredients and developing his repertoire of tools and techniques. Now Eliot was getting ready to open his own restaurant, a fusion place in a trendy part of London where he would showcase all of his culinary expertise, including molecular gastronomy.

Brontë, on the other hand, wasn't very exploratory. At that time she was getting ready to celebrate her ten-year anniversary at the company she had worked for since graduating from university. She was an interior designer, and she'd met Eliot while working on his restaurant space. Brontë's job was to make things comfortable for other people, but she liked to do this for herself too. It made Brontë uncomfortable to 'rock the boat' in any way – at work or at home, and especially in her relationship with Eliot. Recently, Eliot had raised the possibility of them living together. Eliot already spent a lot of time at Brontë's place. In the last few months he had moved utensils and equipment (a sous vide machine and a KitchenAid) into her kitchen and a 'shit ton of recipe books into the living room'. Brontë felt 'uncomfortable' because he was invading her 'space'. But she also said that Eliot 'invaded her headspace' when he wasn't there, and that she missed him and thought about him all the time. I noticed that Brontë talked about space a lot. Suffice to say, she liked her space.

In our session that morning, Brontë told me Eliot had done something that made her feel very distressed on the day their relationship had ended. Brontë had spent all of last week bedridden with a nasty bout of flu. She'd cancelled everything in her diary, including our session. As soon as Eliot heard Brontë was ill, he dropped everything and went straight over to look after her. He brought several bags of fresh ingredients with him and spent all afternoon in the kitchen cooking up a storm. Hours later, Eliot came into Brontë's bedroom holding a tray laden with a large bowl of steaming soup and a freshly baked roll. There was also a paper napkin folded into a swan and a little vase with some flowers from the garden.

The soup Eliot had cooked for Brontë wasn't anything trendy or modernist or molecularly gastronomical. This soup was original, yet traditional, and the recipe had been passed through the generations of Eliot's family. It was his

Jewish grandmother's 'penicillin': chicken soup with matzo balls. This was Eliot's comfort food.

But it was uncomfortable for Brontë.

'I told him straight, no soup was going to make me feel better. Not even his bubbe's,' said Brontë. 'I've never seen chicken soup like that before. He should've just opened a tin.' She looked confused and inconvenienced all at once.

Later that day it was Eliot's turn to be uncomfortable as, for some reason, Brontë's upset about the soup increased. She didn't eat it. She also didn't mince her words about Eliot ('you're an idiot, spending all day making it') or his grandmother ('she's silly calling it "penicillin" because it looks toxic to me'). She threw some gastronomical bombs too, big ones, about the matzo balls ('there are fatty lumps floating around in it') and the soup's greasy, shmaltzy surface ('there's so much oil, maybe the American army will invade the bowl!'). Brontë's verbal attack on Eliot and the soup went on for the entire afternoon. Eliot told her he'd had enough and that he was leaving. Brontë was assailed by her emotions of anger, sadness and fear, so she exploded and said, 'Fine, it's over then'. After he left, she stormed into the bathroom and flushed the soup down the toilet, and all her hopes for their relationship along with it.

Bowlby said that no form of behaviour is accompanied by stronger feeling than attachment behaviour. Or in this case, un-attachment behaviour, which had caused this to become chicken soup not for the soul, but for the hole. Chicken soup is the ultimate comfort food, so what was wrong? Why did it not have the right effect on Brontë? How could it have made her so uncomfortable?

After Brontë had finished describing all the details of the soup showdown, I realised that I had yet another piece of information about Eliot: I now knew his comfort food. But I didn't know hers. So I said: 'Brontë, what is your comfort food?'

I thought she'd have an instant answer, but she didn't. Instead, there was a minute's silence before she responded.

'I don't know,' she said, looking a little lost. 'I don't think I have one.'

I knew the reason why. Her declaration that no soup — or any other food, for that matter — was going to make her feel better was actually true. Comfort food is comforting, but only for those who know the comfort and security of relationships. This has been shown recently in attachment research: that food can be a safe haven, just like a person. The safe haven is, in fact, one of the key ingredients of attachment. I have often seen 'attachment' used as a catch-all term for any and all close relationships. But it isn't. In a scientific sense, an attachment is a relationship bond with some specifics. It's a person who feels like home, a home you can go back to for safety, closeness and comfort when times get tough — a person who is your safe haven — and it's the same with comfort food. One study showed that every-day experiences of loneliness were associated with eating more comfort food, but only for those who had a secure, safe haven in someone. The effect in that experiment was only for comfort food and not just any food participants could get their hands on. Another study found that those secure people also experienced less loneliness by merely writing about their personal comfort food. That's how powerful attachment associations and food can be. And they are always personal. My comfort food is not your comfort food. It also might surprise you to hear not everyone's comfort food is something sugary or stodgy or fatty (some of the comfort foods in that study I just mentioned included kimchi and gyoza – dumplings minus the schmaltz, that is). Even though evolution has beautifully crafted your biology so that eating junk food feels good, that doesn't mean you feel secure. That comes from the association with the person you have that emotional bond with.

Brontë had no comfort food because, unlike Eliot, she had no experience of comfort people – in other words, secure attachments.

But Eliot did. I also knew that about him. Eliot found comfort in his grandmother's soup because she had been a significant part of his childhood. His grandmother (his bubbe) had lived with the family. Eliot's grandmother had been there for him every day when he arrived home from school, and she'd been available for him and responsive to whatever he needed. She was his special attachment figure. Whenever he had been unwell or upset or sad, she made him chicken soup. She gave him care and comfort. Comfort food is never new or strange; it is the comfort of the familiar, just as Bowlby talked about the face of the familiar caregiver for the child. And every time Eliot made the soup now, I imagine he saw his grandmother's reflection glistening in the oily surface. Those weren't just matzo balls bobbing up and down, they were symbolic little lifebuoys. This was more than just a hug in a bowl. This was attachment security in a bowl.

Maybe now you might be thinking about Mum Food from the last chapter. As you may have guessed, that apple pie was Rose's comfort food because of the connection to her mother, her safe haven. Brontë, however, had no such thing. Nobody had been there for her when she was growing up. Her parents ran a bakery together, so life revolved around that, and they weren't at home a lot. Brontë was the 'accident'; she had two sisters who were ten and eleven years older than her, and she was often left in their care. Her sisters would 'forget' to feed her. Brontë remembered making her own food from tins, packets and pots, mostly noodles and soups. Her parents gave her money to buy a hot lunch from the canteen at school, but Brontë would buy crisps, chocolate and sweets from the vending machine instead. As her parents worked long hours at the bakery, they never ate dinner together as a family. Every now and then they would go out at weekends. Brontë remembered one time, just after she'd started school, when they all went to a pub for Sunday lunch. After they had eaten, Brontë went to use the toilet because she had a tummy ache and she stayed in there for a little while. Her family 'just forgot' and left without her. Whenever they drove past this pub, her older sisters would joke, 'That's the pub where we left Brontë behind!' Brontë said that she had always felt a sense of disconnection from her family. She described herself as her 'own little island'.

Since the beginning of their relationship, Eliot had been 'invading' Brontë's island with food. As she put it, 'he eats life'. Brontë could not understand the comfort that food and cooking brought Eliot. She mentioned that one of Eliot's recipe books had 'comfort cooking' in the title, which confused her. For him, food was about attachment, but for her, food was about separation and loss. And there was quite literally a lot of food loss in their relationship, because Brontë never ate much of what Eliot cooked. Forget his fusion stuff: even chicken soup that wasn't from a tin was too exploratory for her. True security means that it is possible to try new things out, without it being make-or-break, but Brontë had never felt this way about anything in life. You need to have enough comfort to leave your comfort zone.

One of the first times I got out of my food comfort zone was at a restaurant run by my father's best friend. Although he had also come to the UK from Cyprus, he ran a French restaurant. To this day, I still have no idea why. We would eat there often when I was a child, and that was where I first had that classic French dessert, îles flottantes (poached meringues floating on a sea of custard). I, of course, expected something that tasted just like Bird's, since that was the only custard I knew. But this custard was so rich, it was almost buttery, and that made me too uncomfortable to eat it. When I was a child, the corner cupboard in our kitchen was essentially a shrine to Bird's desserts: it contained packets of Angel Delight and Dream Topping and the classic instant puddings like custard and semolina, which is what my mother used when she first tried to make my father's favourite dessert, *galaktoboureko*. Despite her best efforts, desserts are not really her thing, and my mother still hasn't mastered that dish. I have witnessed several attempts where the pastry has wibbled a bit, wobbled a lot and then collapsed completely on the plate. My mother's galetoboureko effectively ends up a two-for-one French dessert: when the custard runs out it behaves like a fondant, and since it sits in a sea of custard it looks like an île flottante.

At this French restaurant, because one of my father's attachment figures – his best friend – was right there, he felt secure enough to venture down the culinary road less travelled. Once, my father ordered the very fancy-sounding smoked haddock brandade. He did have pitta with it instead of baguette, which taramasalata-ised it, but still, this was him being exploratory. This is another specific ingredient of attachment, and it's called the secure base. Ainsworth cultivated this concept to explain how you can feel free to explore the world with confidence if you know that care and protection is there from a special someone when needed. As they say in attachment theory: a secure base to go out from, a safe haven to come back to. After my disastrous dessert at the French restaurant that night, my mother provided (or protected) me with the safe haven I needed: we went home and had Bird's custard with Iced Gems on top. To me, that's proper îles flottantes.

At the end of our session that day, Brontë said something which showed me that our comfort food conversation had been the start of building her secure base here in therapy. In fact, what she said was the most exploratory thing I'd heard her say so far: Brontë said that she was going to go home and make herself a chocolate fudge cake from scratch – and 'eat the whole of it.'

That's one way of coping with a separation, I thought to myself.

Brontë didn't believe in comfort cooking, yet at this time of make-or-break, she was choosing to bake? I was curious about where this was coming from. Brontë said she hadn't spoken to Eliot since the soup incident, but that every evening she had found herself picking up and reading one of his many recipe books. Although Brontë was clear about why she was making the chocolate fudge cake ('The recipe says this is what you make when you've been chucked'), she wasn't sure why she was reading the recipe books.

She was comfort reading. This was about her seeking out her safe haven.

'I wonder if you're wanting to be close to Eliot. They're his books, after all. They're associated with him,' I said.

'Possibly. I am really starting to miss him,' admitted Brontë.

Now is the time to tell you about the other key ingredient of attachment, in addition to the safe haven and secure base. It's actually anxiety: when your attachment figure is unexpectedly not there for you, separation anxiety is experienced. This is the stuff of a broken heart.

It turned out Brontë hadn't been 'chucked'. It wasn't over. Eliot missed her just as much. So this story, and their story, ended up uncomfortably ever after. Brontë and Eliot decided to work on their relationship in couples' therapy. They figured out the space between them. Because that's what the secure base and the safe haven are about: space. If you boil it down, attachment behaviour involves either going away from, or back to, your 'home' base. There is a special type of couples' therapy based on attachment theory. It's called Emotionally Focused Therapy – and it's just that. Brontë and Eliot learned how to focus on, and tune into, the emotions that were at the heart of the distress in their relationship. This helped them to support each other. They learned how to be each other's safe havens.

In her individual therapy, Brontë began to work through her own emotional soup. As she did so, she discovered that 'her space', with anyone she ever got close to, was a pseudo-safe haven, created for control, not connection. After all, if we don't trust something or someone, we try to control it. It was her way of keeping herself protected. It was an old attachment strategy, and it was getting in the way of her new relationship with Eliot. But as we started to make sense of Brontë's attachment story in therapy, she felt safe to let go of that behaviour. As her trust – her secure bases – built with both me and Eliot, Brontë began to feel more confident to get out of her comfort zone. She felt freer to take chances and explore choices, and this is exactly what therapy is about. And along the way, Brontë got more comfortable with Eliot's homemade chicken soup.

But she still preferred tinned.

* * *

Avgolemoni

I have no idea whether the chicken or the egg came first. But in this soup, comfort comes first.

Serves 4

1 medium-sized chicken (or you could use a couple of poussins)
2 teaspoons salt
230g pudding rice (approximately one large mug full)
3 large eggs
Freshly squeezed juice of 1 lemon, strained

Put the chicken in a large saucepan and cover with cold water. Add one teaspoon of the salt. Bring it to the boil over a high heat, then reduce the heat to medium. Simmer the chicken for about an hour, or until cooked all the way through, skimming off any scum that rises to the surface with a large metal spoon.

Carefully remove the chicken from the water, which is now your stock. Set the chicken aside to cool.

Rinse the rice in a sieve with cold running water. Bring the chicken stock to the boil and add the rice and the other teaspoon of salt. Reduce the heat and simmer for 15 minutes, until the rice is tender.

In the meantime, whisk the eggs in a large heatproof bowl until they are frothy.

Once the rice is cooked, turn off the heat. Whisk the lemon juice into the eggs. Then, whisk in a ladleful of the hot stock (the cooked rice will have sunk to the bottom, so it will be easy to ladle off the liquid only). Once it's incorporated into the egg and lemon mixture, whisk in another ladleful of stock. Repeat twice more until you have a frothy, eggy-lemony stock.

Tip this stock back into the saucepan with the rice and stir until everything is fully combined. The soup is now ready to serve (if you need to reheat it, do so very gently, otherwise the eggs will scramble). I usually flake some of the boiled chicken into my bowl, but you can have the meat as a side dish to the soup, along with bread, of course.

3

The Strange Situation of the Dinner Table

*What do you do when you fear
the person you love?*

Have you seen the film *Heartburn?* It stars Meryl Streep
and Jack Nicholson, and it's based on the book of the same
name by Nora Ephron. In case you're a stranger to the
story, it's a thinly disguised novel about Nora's relationship with her husband Carl Bernstein, who is best known
for reporting on the Watergate scandal for the *Washington
Post*. I would say *Heartburn* is probably the best book I have
ever read about marriage – and food. There is a lot of talk
about mashed potatoes and salad vinaigrettes, and there are
recipes too. (I think it's interesting that there isn't a recipe
for Watergate Salad, but maybe that's because it's not really
a salad and it has no vinaigrette: it's made with pistachio
pudding mix, tinned pineapple, mini marshmallows, nuts
and instant whip.) In *Heartburn*, Nora works her recipes
peripherally into the chapters. Don't ask me how, but she
even gets food into the group therapy scenes, which works
because, fittingly, it's food for the suffering (chopped liver).

But that is not Nora Ephron's greatest achievement. She also wrote the screenplay for the film, for which she created scenes that are not in the book. My favourite is a dinner scene with Meryl Streep's character, Rachel, who is married to Jack Nicholson's character, Mark, where they're in a restaurant with friends playing the 'who you are' game: each person at the table has to list five words to describe who they are. Whenever I watch a film, I would usually be more interested in what's going into the characters' mouths, food-wise, rather than what's coming out, words-wise. I did notice that during the game, a lot of deep-fried food was delivered to the table, including a gigantic tangle of crispy onion strings and battered jumbo shrimp. However, this time it was the word game that whet my appetite.

Why?

Because by using that game in the scene, Nora unconsciously (or consciously, who knows) manages to reference one of the most powerful research tools in attachment theory. That five-word-description technique features in the Adult Attachment Interview, which is mostly used in research studies, but can sometimes help with therapy practice. In this interview, a person is asked to provide five adjectives or words that reflect their childhood relationship with each parent, and to say why they chose each one. They are also asked about experiences of rejections, separations and losses, and what happened when they were upset, hurt or ill as a child. The interview focuses a lot on the past, but there are also questions about what the person's relationships with their parents are like now, as well as a question about the future and what their three wishes for their own child would be twenty years from now. One of the aims of the Adult Attachment Interview is to, as researchers put it, 'surprise the unconscious'. As you can imagine, the interview gets you to reflect on things you might not necessarily think about every day.

There's also another interview I have used in a lot in my research, called the Attachment Style Interview. That focuses more on present relationships, the three people you are closest to and how you seek support from them. You can think of these two interviews as two slightly different recipes for the same dish, which have distinct techniques in their methods. One is about how you talk about your relationships; the other is about what you do in your relationships. The important thing is that you come out with the same dish, comprising two words, which is about how you connect with other people: your attachment style.

These days, people talk about attachment styles a lot – and not in an unconscious-Nora-Ephron-movie-dinner-scene way. The categories used in research often, and quite consciously, find their way into other aspects of life. When I'm at a dinner party, I have found that someone will say 'my partner isn't securely attached' before I've even had a chance to ask them to pass the salt. Your attachment style can either be secure or insecure. But it's important to keep in mind that these are merely labels; it's what's going on underneath that matters. That's where my own research began. I have never had the 'who are you?' question at a dinner party, but when I'm asked 'what do you do?', my answer is always a lot more than five words because I go back to the start; I tell people about my background in biology, which is what I first did in attachment research. If we're eating something by then, I'll throw in a fun fact and say that, much like we have a digestive system that is working its magic right there and then, we also have an attachment 'system'. You can't point to it literally in your body but its function is the same as any other biological system – it helps us to live. Don't get me wrong, love is a very lovely part of human life, but attachments aren't for fun – they are for survival. In times of stress and threat, your attachment system is switched on and it has one set goal: to seek closeness to your attachment figure, so that you can feel comforted, safe and secure.

But what if your attachment system doesn't work so well, or securely? You'll either get anxious, so you'll seek a lot of closeness in some way, or you'll completely avoid closeness in any way. Much of my own research has examined these insecure attachment styles. There are also subcategories of anxious and avoidant insecure attachment styles, depending on what you do if you can't turn to your loved one for help during times of distress – that is to say, if you don't have a safe haven. This is where F-words are important: fight (angry-dismissive style), flight (fearful style), fawn (enmeshed/preoccupied style), forget (withdrawn style). All of these F-words are strategies for trying to survive, or at the very least, trying to make something hurt less. The problem is they don't really make you feel secure. That's why they're called insecure.

In my own family, I have come up with different ways of describing attachment styles, especially for my relatives in Cyprus, for whom some words get a little lost in translation. For preoccupied/enmeshed, I use a well-known Greek phrase: three words that, in my opinion, nail it: *kolos kai vraki*. It means 'arse and underwear' and describes relationships where people are so close, they're inseparable, much like underwear is to an arse. This, perhaps unsurprisingly, my family can understand. After all, research has found that when it comes to insecure attachment, the anxious style has a higher rate than the avoidant type in Mediterranean countries, likely because of their more collectivist cultural values. And because 'we' rather than 'I' is emphasised in that part of the world, this is probably also why food sharing works so well for these folks. One study found that those who have an avoidant attachment style avoid sharing food with anyone, whether it's a romantic partner or a friend or family. The same experiment showed that attachment anxiety is associated with more food-sharing behaviour, especially accepting food from others. I guess this explains my family's style of eating meze, where things are put onto your plate whether you want them or not.

The dinner table is a bit of a strange place in my family. But for my patient Leonard, it was another situation altogether.

Leonard wanted therapy because he said he had recently become more 'withdrawn'. He wasn't identifying his avoidant attachment style with that word; it was just an incidental use of an adjective to tell me why he'd come to see me. Leonard reminded me of some research I had carried out on attachment styles in children. In that work, a certain animal was used to describe each insecure style: the withdrawn tortoise who goes into their shell and tries to forget, the enmeshed monkey who fawns and clings, the angry-dismissive grizzly bear who fights and the fearful deer who flees. There was something quite childlike about Leonard. He was also like a withdrawn tortoise. He looked older than his mid-forties; it was as though he was an old man in a young man's body. He had a boyish smile and was toothless in places. Leonard could have given any tortoise a run for its money, movement-wise. He moved very slowly. His most tortoise-like feature, however, was his hunched upper body, which made it look like he was carrying the weight of the world on his shoulders.

Leonard was withdrawn with words, too. For the first weeks of our work I tried to draw him out slowly by using lots of adjectives to name his feelings. Therapy has been called the 'talking cure', but with Leonard there was very little talking in the sessions – hardly any words, feelings or memories. Leonard simply said he couldn't remember things. But his memory lapses felt like more than mere forgetfulness. It was as though he'd gone to some faraway place. Sometimes I got the feeling that Leonard wanted to go, even right at the start of our session. And then at the end, when it was time to go, he couldn't move any more slowly. His behaviours felt conflicted and confused.

One day, I decided to ask Leonard that question from the Adult Attachment Interview, in the hope that we might get at least five words in our fifty-minute session. I said: 'Leonard, I'm wondering if you could choose five words that reflect your relationship with your mother in childhood?'

I think *my* unconscious was a little surprised that Leonard didn't dismiss my question. He sat back in his chair and stroked his chin as he thought about his answer.

In the meantime, I started to compile my own list of five words. Therapist. Trying really hard. Hungry.

My last adjective was interesting to me. I realised I often felt hungry in my sessions with Leonard, but there was no physical reason why I should be. By the time I saw Leonard for our session at 11.30 a.m. I had generally eaten and drunk at least eleven things (espresso first thing, then toast and egg and avocado and tomatoes, followed by some berries and a dollop of Greek yoghurt, washed down with orange juice. Then, as I arrived for Leonard's appointment at the clinic, I'd grab another coffee and granola bar for elevenses from the café next door. Then

I'd eat a sweetie or two from the bowl in the waiting room). I wondered if I was picking up on another kind of hunger from him.

After about five minutes, five words came out of Leonard's mouth: 'Wife. Cook. Quiet. Dinner table.'

'Dinner table?' I said, slightly taken aback by his choice. Perhaps his mother was sturdy and table-like, a bit like the American chef Julia Child. I asked Leonard to say more about his last two words.

'Every night at 6.30 p.m. like clockwork. Dinner time,' said Leonard. Then, off his own back, he added a couple of adjectives: 'I had a normal, happy childhood, because we ate dinner together at the table every night.'

Leonard was not the only person I knew who invested the dinner table with a lot of emotional power. Nigella Lawson was so taken by this piece of furniture that she named one of her books after it. In the introduction of *At My Table*, she says that when she moved into her first home, before she did anything else, she bought a table. Nigella talks about a table as something not just to eat at, but to live around.

Leonard's table comment certainly said something about the attachment world he lived in. Given that the five-words game was drawing Leonard out a little, I thought I'd strike again while the iron was hot.

'How about your father, Leonard? If you could choose five words that reflect your relationship with him in childhood?' I said.

This time Leonard's five words arrived a lot more quickly: 'He was like Gordon Ramsay.'

At that moment, I saw Leonard cower. His shoulders curved even more than usual. He was frightened and I felt it, like the sizzle you get when you put fresh meat on the barbecue. Then he said, so quietly that I almost missed it, 'He would shout and swear a lot.'

Leonard's body also remembered something about dinner time. 'I used to get butterflies in my tummy before dinner, so I must have looked forward to it,' he said. His words came out a little louder, but they weren't very convincing. I tried to imagine Leonard's idyllic family dinner scene – a country kitchen with butterflies floating around and a table dressed in gingham cloth – but instead I had five words, including an F-word, about his father in my mind: *I bet he's fucking scary*. I was also curious about Leonard's choice of metaphor; I wondered if the butterflies were really knots of stress, rather than happiness or excitement. To make sure I wasn't getting the wrong end of the stick, and in the hope that Leonard might elaborate a bit more, I repeated back what he'd just told me.

'So, you looked forward to dinner time at the table?' I said.

'I was at school all day, my dad was out at work and my mum was at home. Dinner was the only time we would ever come together,' said Leonard.

So far, so average. But this dinner table was a Strange Situation.

41

I'm not using a metaphor. The Strange Situation is, in fact, the original attachment tool – it came out before the interviews and before Nora Ephron married Carl Bernstein. The Strange Situation was Ainsworth's baby. It was part of her observation research on mothers and babies, and the patterns of attachment that were first found here have paved the way for all the work on adult attachment styles since. It's a laboratory experiment that is done with children from around the time they are a year old (typically no later than two), and so-called because it involves something that is very strange for a child: separation from their parent. The Strange Situation assesses the different ways in which children attach to their caregivers based on two things: how they respond to separation and reunion. In other words, goodbye and hello.

In Leonard's early life, the dinner table was a place of reunion after a day of separation from his parents. Food writers and anthropologists understand this, and much has been written about dinner as a unique time that brings family members together after being apart during the day. Dinner at the table is an event bounded in time and space. It has rituals and rules of interaction; not least is the consistent slot it has in the day, which gives it something in common with therapy. My favourite food writer, Laurie Colwin (those are six words I'll probably use again in this book), who wrote *Home Cooking*, discusses the family table and says that 'some time in the day we need to disconnect, reconnect, and look around us.' That's a pretty spot-on definition of the Strange Situation. And in Ainsworth's experiment it was indeed the reconnection, the reunion, that mattered most of all.

For the rest of our session, Leonard and I stayed with the table, and he talked about what these reunions were like. Leonard's father treated dinner time as family-style force-feeding. He would pile things on Leonard's plate (mostly extra vegetables) and he would help himself to things from Leonard's plate that he wanted for himself (usually Leonard's favourite – roast potatoes – which he used to save until last). However, his father would never share his food; he would joke that what was on his plate was 'mine-all-mine'. Leonard's father would yell at him for eating without cutlery. Leonard even had to eat his bread and butter with a knife and fork. His father would also shout at him to stop eating side dishes that might fill him up, like bread and butter. Sometimes Leonard's father would throw food at him, as though he was an animal, and when things fell on the floor, Leonard had to pick up the items and eat them. If his father felt that Leonard had eaten enough, he wouldn't let him have dessert, which was Leonard's favourite part of the meal. On one occasion only, Leonard had protested, which had made his father even angrier. He had shouted at Leonard, 'I'll make you a pudding!' His father then grabbed the squirty cream and sprayed it all over Leonard's head and put a cherry on top. Then he said, 'There, I've made you a pudding!'

I was truly horrified. But Leonard laughed a little laugh, which felt like a peculiar response. It was like he wasn't letting himself be conscious of how horrible this behaviour was from the person who was supposed to be his caregiver. It was indeed Hell's Kitchen table. If it were me, I would have hidden underneath it or run for cover, which probably says a lot about my own attachment style.

In *At My Table*, Nigella Lawson also mentions my favourite M. F. K. Fisher quote, the one about food, love and security being entwined. Nigella says that these three things meet around the table.

I wasn't so sure that was happening at Leonard's childhood dinner table.

At that point in the session we had a really long silence. There was tension in the room, so much that you could have cut it with a knife. But there was one thing I wanted to know, so I broke the silence.

'Leonard, what did you do after that incident with your father?' I said.

'Nothing. I just sat still at the table,' he said.

There was Leonard's F-word: freeze.

The Leonard who was sitting in the chair opposite me now was the same child who'd sat there at the dinner table: he was detached and disconnected. His body was there, but his mind was not. I also noticed he had his hand over his mouth.

Then, five words about Leonard's attachment style entered my mind: *oh my God, he's disorganised.*

In the Strange Situation, Ainsworth described one pattern of secure attachment and two patterns of insecure attachment, which she called 'avoidant' and 'resistant' (that's 'anxious' in the adult world of attachment styles). However, there were some children that didn't quite fit these categories. During the reunion part of the Strange Situation, these children showed some really odd and contradictory and seemingly inexplicable behaviours. After some more research, Ainsworth's colleague, Mary Main, added another category: 'disorganised'. Adults can have a disorganised attachment style too, which can be determined from the two interviews I mentioned earlier. Main also played a big part in developing the Adult Attachment Interview, and the genius 'five words' question.

The thing is, insecure attachment styles might be insecure, but they are organised, in the sense that they are only one thing: either avoidance or anxiety. The disorganised style mixes and mingles both: a person is anxious on the inside and avoidant on the outside. Can you see how messy that is? It's oppositional. Push and pull. A bit like turning up the heat and trying to cool down something at the same time. There's no tidy, organised strategy. That's really what attachment styles are – they are strategies to help you adapt to your environment. Bowlby was quite the evolutionist at heart and, as he said, all behaviour makes sense in context. Leonard and I were discovering that, in his context – the dinner table – being strategy-less, sitting still and freezing was all he could do to survive in the face of something else that made no sense: how the person who was supposed to love and care for him could hurt him. It was impossible for Leonard to turn his attachment system off, but that meant he was seeking closeness to the same person who was causing him distress. He was in a double bind. As attachment theory would say, Leonard's caregiver was his scaregiver. A disorganised attachment style has fear at its heart, and Leonard's fear was here in the therapy room right now. Acknowledging all of this was scary, so I could understand why he was trying to keep himself and his picture of a normal, happy childhood safe. In reality, this table was the place where food, estrangement and insecurity met.

One of Ainsworth's most important findings from her research was that it's not attachment per se, but the security of attachment that is affected by a parent's sensitivity. It's not about whether you will attach (because you will – that's about biology and evolution and survival), but about how well you attach. Attachment is affected by presence – being physically there, which the dinner table was for Leonard. But that's not enough. Attachment security is affected by being emotionally there – in other words, by sensitivity, which was not at Leonard's table. The word 'sensitivity' doesn't simply mean warmth, tenderness and fuzziness. Ainsworth's was a technical definition that meant having an awareness of the signals and signs in the child's behaviour, interpreting them accurately and responding to them appropriately and promptly. So sensitivity isn't only about what you do. It's also about what you don't do.

Which brings us to the other person at Leonard's dinner table: his mother.

Sometimes it's not the person who caused us harm with whom we feel most angry – it's the one who didn't protect us. Leonard's mother had been 'quiet' and I wondered if Leonard was keeping his anger quiet and withdrawn, and expressing it in dismissiveness instead. I had a feeling that Leonard's mother was also disorganised. One of Main's most significant discoveries was that a mother's Adult Attachment Interview category is strongly related to her child's Strange Situation category. Leonard's mother had been there at the table. But she hadn't been there for him. Leonard had never had a safe haven or a secure base. Perhaps that's what I could be for him, once a therapeutic relationship was established.

By the end of our session, I think both mine and Leonard's unconscious were surprised at the situation our conversation had uncovered. I knew there were still a lot of feelings to un-freeze, and to organise. But what I did know was that our dinner table talk had helped me start to see who Leonard was. And there was nothing strange about that.

* * *

Ouzo Calamari

This is inspired by that very special scene in the film *Heartburn* where there is deep-fried food on the table and attachment theory in the conversation. Rachel and Mark had battered shrimp in the movie, but my fried seafood of choice would always be calamari. For cultural connection, I've used ouzo in this recipe – its high alcohol content also makes for a really light and crisp coating. A spritz of lemon before serving complements the subtle aniseed flavour nicely.

Serves 2

500g cleaned squid
125ml ouzo (or you could use vodka or gin)
70g plain flour
30g cornflour
½ teaspoon bicarbonate of soda
¼ teaspoon salt
100ml sparkling water
Rapeseed oil, vegetable oil or groundnut oil, for
    deep frying
Lemon wedge and sea salt flakes, to serve

Cut the squid into 1cm rings, leaving any tentacles as they are. Put them in a bowl with 75ml of the ouzo and leave to marinate for 15–20 minutes.

In a large bowl, mix the plain flour, cornflour, bicarbonate of soda, salt, sparkling water and the rest of the ouzo until fully combined and smooth in texture.

Heat the oil in a deep-fat fryer or a deep saucepan. For the latter you will need to ensure that the oil comes about halfway up the side of the pan and use a medium-high heat. For both methods, the temperature of the oil for frying will need to be around 180°C. If you don't have a thermometer you can test whether the oil is hot enough by carefully dipping a cube of stale bread or the end of a wooden spoon into it. It should bubble steadily but not vigorously.

When you are ready to cook, line a shallow bowl or plate with a few sheets of paper towel. Drain the squid, and ensure the squid bowl, the batter bowl, and the fryer or the pan are all in close proximity.

Pat the squid dry using paper towel. Put it in the batter bowl and move the pieces around to ensure they are all coated evenly.

Time to fry! Working quickly and carefully, place the pieces of battered squid into the oil, in batches. Do not overcrowd the fryer or the pan because this will reduce the temperature, and the squid will steam rather than fry. Fry for 1–2 minutes, or until they are crisp and golden.

Carefully remove the squid from the oil with a slotted spoon or tongs and place onto the paper towel-lined plate to drain the excess oil. Spritz with lemon juice, sprinkle with a few sea salt flakes and serve immediately.

4

'Stressed' Spelled Backwards is 'Desserts'

Who can you talk to in tough times?

Can you think of the last time something stressful happened to you? When life didn't go to plan, and you felt out of control and alone in this strange world? It happened to me recently. I mentioned earlier that I am likely to seek out my mother when things go wrong in the kitchen. This was exactly the case one Saturday evening a few months ago when I invited people over for dinner. An hour before they arrived, I was making the white sauce for this Greek dish I cook quite often for friends, and it ended up, well, let's just say, wrong. I video-called my mother and showed her my lumpy sauce. She could see my teary face, which from all the stress had become a little lumpy too, and very red. My mother listened, comforted me and reassured me that running to the supermarket to buy a jar of Dolmio's creamy lasagne sauce was not the answer. I've mentioned that my mother loves convenience foods, but that jarred stuff is too processed even for her. We used it once out of curiosity when I was a child. Their television advertisement asked,

'When'sa your Dolmio day?' My mother said never again after that.

On the phone that Saturday, after we replayed the revolting Dolmio memory, my mother shared her seasoned kitchen know-how with me. It gave me the secure base I needed to confidently sieve the sauce and cook on. It was attachment in (culinary) action.

And so, the last time you were stressed, in the kitchen or otherwise, hopefully you turned to a trusted family member or a friend to help.

Or perhaps, like my patient Jack, you ate a dessert.

I met Jack in therapy when he was in his sixties. He was a large man, with forget-me-not blue eyes that twinkled and winked too, sometimes. The dessert Jack ate when he was stressed was made by his wife of forty years, Angelica, the love of his life. Or, as he would say in booming cockney rhyming slang, his 'treacle tart' (FYI, treacle tart is not the dessert in his story). I discovered it meant 'sweetheart', and it was one of the many phrases I learned from Jack. After a few sessions I taught Jack a word too, one that I thought might resonate with him. I know a fair bit of German, so when Jack told me his dessert story, I mentioned *Kummerspeck* to him: it translates as 'grief bacon' and refers to the way we sometimes use food to soothe our stress. But Jack never ate bacon, or any other food, when he was stressed. He would only ever eat this particular pudding.

Before I talk about the dessert Jack ate, I want to talk about stress. Stress is my area of expertise. I don't do it well personally (as I've just shown with my white sauce crisis), but I do professionally, and it all started many years ago with my PhD, which was about attachment and stress.

For the attachment part of my research, I would interview participants, but stress was studied in a very different way: my participants had to give saliva samples that I would analyse in the lab. I needed them to spit for me to assess the stress hormone cortisol. You have cortisol in almost every cell of your body, but asking people for saliva in research is easier than asking them to give you any other bodily fluid, especially when they are stressed.

It's very easy to stress people out. The same things that stress you in life stress you in a laboratory, and cause cortisol to rise. These are unfamiliarity, lack of control and worrying people are going to judge you negatively, which is the most powerful of them all. The reason for that is fairly simple – and very old. Once upon a time, when we lived in tribes, being judged badly by our fellow tribe members would have had serious consequences for safety and survival. I'll be the first to say that Greeks can be melodramatic, but in the early days of civilisation they weren't wrong to consider exile and death as equivalent punishments. After all, your chances of dealing with a predator are much better if you're not alone.

Luckily, we don't face physical threats like that any-more. Life has moved forwards. But our brains and bodies haven't. Nowadays, a psychological threat, like negative judgement, rejection or criticism, will still trigger the same old biological stress system and fight-or-flight responses. The reason remains the same: we want attachment, not sep-aration and loss. So, how attached you are and how stressed you are go hand in hand. As I saw in my own research, cortisol spikes continually if you feel insecure in your rela-tionships. Cortisol running rampant around your body all the time will have disastrous effects – that kind of chronic stress is physically not good for you. Therefore, as my col-league David Sbarra from the University of Arizona says, every day you should cultivate the heck out of your rela-tionships for your health. As this is a book about food, the natural comparison for me to give you is that good-quality, non-stressful relationships are as important for your health as eating a good diet. Science shows this, hands down.

Still, there's nothing wrong with eating a dessert.

Just not when you're stressed.

Eating a dessert during stress is actually quite a back-wards thing to do. Biologically, stress eating makes no sense. Death by chocolate may be the name of a cake but it is, in fact, a very real possibility. It's just not sensible to be sitting there stuffing your face with a chocolate bar, or any other food, when your brain is telling you that you're about to be eaten by a lion. Stress promotes survival behaviours, so your body needs to prioritise and mobilise. To help this happen, we have those classic stress responses, such as sweaty hands, dry mouth, dilated pupils, rapid breathing and a racing heart to get you going. This is the time for fight or flight; feed is not the F-word here because you can't digest food easily when you're stressed. Your body's 'rest-and-digest' system will take care of desserts, as well as other foods, when you're a little more relaxed.

Speaking of which, there was some chocolate in Jack's stress dessert, in the form of cocoa powder lovingly sprinkled on by Angelica. Jack seemed to really like chocolate, and sweets too. On several occasions, at the start of our session Jack would offer me a piece of whatever confectionary he had bought from the shop next to the clinic. It was often Rolos, which I always politely declined because I don't like gooey caramel. There was no question about who Jack would give his last Rolo to, of course: it would be Angelica, whom he'd met when he was a teenager. Jack was a cheeky chappy from the East End, while Angelica was from the east of Italy. Her parents were first-generation Italian immigrants who moved to London in the 1950s when Angelica was a child. They ran a café that served an Anglo-Italian menu of various cooked breakfasts and homemade pastas. When Angelica left school, she started to work at the café full-time. This was where she and Jack first set eyes on each other. He would visit for breakfast (his order was a sausage sandwich with tomato ketchup) and lunch (usually a cheese and pickle sandwich). He would pop by for a cup of tea, too, in the afternoon.

The café closed at 3.30 p.m. and if Jack was there, Angelica would package up leftovers for him (he loved their meaty lasagne and the spinach and ricotta cannelloni). They often stayed at the café, chatting until the evening. You could say those were their first dates. Jack eventually asked Angelica out on an official date, and their courtship quickly became an engagement. Jack said he'd known all along that he and Angelica would become husband and wife.

'That movie, *Jerry Maguire*, it was like that. She had me at hello. Or ciao,' said Jack. He clearly had a soft and gooey inside that could rival any chocolate bar when it came to Angelica. Jack enjoyed talking about his relationship in therapy. It was clear they loved each other very much. Angelica would call Jack 'her love, her amore', but as Jack told me this in the session, his cockney command of Italian made it sound like he was telling his burly mate Ray that he wanted seconds: ''ey, more Ray'.

Jack found his joie de vivre with Angelica. His life now had so much more colour compared to previously. So did his food: his sausage sandwich now contained sundried toma-toes, his cheese and pickle sandwich was now made with mozzarella, and both were on ciabatta. Before Angelica, Jack's food life was beige, and had been since the cradle, and even earlier. Flavour is learned in the womb. When Jack came into the world, chips and sliced white bread and but-ter were foods he was already familiar with. Occasionally, if there was leftover mashed potato, Jack's mother would make bubble and squeak (I had to check that Jack meant the traditional British dish, and that he wasn't trying to indicate our cultural differences. Before Jack, 'bubble and squeak' for 'Greek' was the only cockney rhyming slang I knew).

As a child, Jack and his parents would eat dinner on trays in front of the television, mostly in silence. 'We didn't talk about anything,' he said. 'We just got on with it, especially my mother. She was run ragged with long shifts at the hospital.' Jack's mother was a nurse in the NHS, so naturally her job was very stressful. Given that we also experience stress in the womb, I wondered if Jack had been affected even before he was born. Jack's father also had a pressurised job – he was a policeman. His parents smoked and drank to manage their stress. They didn't support each other, or their son. Jack said he couldn't remember a time when his mother or father asked him how he was. So he coped by 'keeping himself to himself'.

This was what made Angelica different from Jack's family, as well as his friends, who just thought of him as 'Jack the lad'. Angelica saw past that, and wanted to get to know the real Jack.

'I never had anyone to talk to before Angelica,' Jack said. 'From the start, I could be myself with her, you know? The good, the bad and the ugly. I ain't pretty when I'm stressed, which I was a lot at work, and she would see that side of me.'

'Can you say more about that? It sounds important,' I said.

'Well, you know, I would tell her all about the pressure. Working for the London Fire Brigade wasn't easy. Every day you never knew what you were going to be faced with. It wasn't only fire calls; it could have been a road traffic incident or a medical emergency. Rescuing cats in trees was even really stressful. And then there was the responsibility of being station manager. Whenever there was something wrong, Angelica always had time to talk. She would stop whatever she was doing and say, "Amore, I've put the kettle on. Let's talk and have tea. To cheer you up!" And she meant literally,' said Jack.

It sounded like a nice ritual, and I knew first-hand how comforting tea could be. I also remember reading about a study during my PhD that showed how tea helped to speed up recovery from a stressful experience by bringing cortisol levels back to normal. So tea really can soothe stress away.

'So you and Angelica would have tea together? And talk about the stresses of work over that?' I said, simply paraphrasing to let Jack know I was listening.

'Yes, we'd have tea — you know, T E A — and we'd have it as T I for tiramisu,' he said.

Tiramisu was Jack's dessert.

'Right, I see,' I said.

'In Italian, you see, tiramisu means "cheer me up" or "pick me up", because that's what the caffeine does,' said Jack. 'Angelica always made it when I was having stress at work. She knew it was my favourite. We would sit there talking, drinking tea and eating her lovely tiramisu. It always made me feel better. It's like they say, a problem shared is a problem halved. With her it always was,' Jack smiled from his tummy. He always looked full and nourished when he spoke about Angelica.

Tiramisu is a classic Italian trifle-like dessert made of sponge finger biscuits soaked in sweet coffee and liqueur, layered with a mixture of whipped eggs, mascarpone and cream, dusted with cocoa. While the traditional English jelly-and-custard trifle has pretty mundane origins, having been born from using up stale leftovers, tiramisu has a sexy history. It was apparently invented about 100 years ago, around the same time as attachment theory. As Bowlby was discovering what keeps people attached, the brothels of Treviso in northern Italy were finding out that tiramisu kept tired clients going for longer and paying for more sex.

This is when eating a dessert does make sense. A heavily caffeinated one, that is.

But for Jack, although eating a dessert might have been backwards from a biological stress perspective, his tiramisu was really about seeking out and talking to Angelica. So in terms of attachment, it was the best, most helpful and for-wards thing Jack could do when he was stressed.

My own experience of stress and desserts is slightly different to Jack's. Years ago, I went to Leiths School of Food and Wine school to do an intensive course in classic French cuisine. It was a bit of a baptism of fire, to say the least. Whenever we had a practical test, we would wait outside the kitchens, shaking in our catering clogs about whatever culinary task was ahead. If there had been someone peddling diazepam in the queue, I'm sure they would have made a killing. There was a lot of judgement. At the first pastry practical, my teacher measured the cracks in my shortcrust pastry with a ruler and counted the redcurrants on each sprig that garnished my fruit tart.

But there were also several stressful times that didn't involve desserts. In the knife skills lesson, I simply could not master the rolling chop technique. To be honest, I didn't understand what the big deal was. People chop in all sorts of ways, don't they? The mothers and the grandmothers in my family have always held fruit and vegetables in their hands and chopped them in mid-air without an ounce of trouble, and with nothing more than a cheap melamine-handled table knife. No rolling, and not a chopping board in sight. When I tried to explain the term for cutting vegetables into thin, matchstick-sized pieces to my aunt Antigone in Cyprus, she responded, 'Why would a carrot pretend to be a woman called Julienne?'

During one of the practical tests on meat, I found out that some of my culinary know-how was no-go. On that day, the recipe was smoky chilli with black beans, served with rice – but I decided to add a dollop of extrapolation. I figured that if you are supposed to boil pasta in water as salty as the sea, you should do the same with rice. You shouldn't. My teacher had to spit my rice out.

And then I set the kitchen on fire in the middle of my final exam.

I can feel my body initiating a stress response as I relive the memory while writing this, so I'll give you the brief version of that story, in the form of a tip: never leave your chicken breast wrapped in parchment paper next to the stove with the flame turned up to highest-high. Because it will catch fire.

On the bright side, if there is a fire in the kitchen, you will find that chef's clogs, however ugly they may be, are really useful. After my teacher stomped the fire out, there was a pile of ashy flakes on the floor. With my whole pounding heart, I stood there wishing a phoenix would rise from them. It didn't. The only thing rising at that moment were my cortisol levels.

I was mortified. I experienced what felt like the most mortification that could happen to a human being. My mind and body were mortified to cinders, like my chicken. The episode included all the ingredients of stress, the most powerful being that — like the crack-measuring and the rice-spitting — it happened in front of the whole class. My mind was flooded with thoughts of everyone's negative judgements, ranging from 'she's a crap cook' to 'let's re-baptise the place Leiths School of Food and Fire'.

It goes without saying that I did a lot of talking about this with my therapist at the time. Even though things worked out and I ended up getting a distinction, my self-esteem had sunk like a bad soufflé. I needed help talking through and making sense of all the feelings that came up in the kitchen that day. What I was doing was confiding, and this is the kind of talking that happens in therapy.

It was the same type of talking that Jack did with Angelica over tiramisu.

Cast your mind back to the attachment styles I talked about in chapter three. The insecure styles are all about our responses to stress and threat: fight, flight, fawn, forget, freeze. But there is also a secure F-word strategy: *find* someone to talk to. It's the seeking out that I mentioned at the start of this chapter. Psychologists call this response to stress tend-and-befriend. It's about affiliation and attachment and, accordingly, relates to the body's 'anti-stress hormone', oxytocin. You might have heard of oxytocin as the 'hug hormone' due to its associations with attachment and food behaviours, including breast-feeding and feeling full. Oxytocin has also been linked to increased libido, which I guess gives it something in common with the tiramisu in Treviso.

Attachment theory says that you don't seek out simply anyone when you're stressed. You may have many special people in your life whom you love and want to be close to, but there is something extra that turns an affectional bond into an attachment bond. That is, when you are stressed, you seek security and comfort from that particular relationship. Babies do this physically, by crawling or clinging to their caregiver. As adults, this becomes more psychological, and the equivalent seeking out of our loved one is confiding. Years ago, my own research study found that confiding was so important that it predicted participants' stress hormones: more confiding equalled lower stress hormone levels.

The more Jack confided in Angelica, the less stressed he felt. The thing is, while he was talking and filling his tummy with tiramisu, he wasn't simply getting stuff off his chest. That is not confiding. That is venting, which isn't always helpful, even if it does feel cathartic. In fact, research shows that sharing negative emotions in this way can increase stress in your body. This is because it's strategy-less: the emotion is expressed and nothing is done with it.

Confiding has something additional attached to it. What you are seeking is someone to help you with your distress. Research reveals that confiding works for your wellbeing by helping you to feel you can cope. Bowlby himself said that attachment behaviours were part of the child's capacity to cope with stress. And you don't change as an adult: help-seeking is at the heart of confiding. What you need is someone to be there, but their support needs to be more than just 'there there'. If you share with someone who doesn't challenge you to rethink things, it's no more helpful than talking to yourself or not talking at all. Sometimes, someone else can see what you don't, as Jack discovered when he confided in Angelica.

'When we talked, she would help me see things in a different way, through her eyes. Her mince pies were lovely,' he said, looking wistful.

As my mind imagined an Italian version of a mince pie filled with dried fruit encased in panettone-like pastry, Jack told me that 'mince pies' meant 'eyes'.

It was not the only part of Angelica that was lovely. Jack went on to tell me more.

'Angelica listened to whatever I was saying. She never judged me. You know the things they say about men having feelings, the stigma, like you're not a real man, that you're weak if you're a bit emotional. God help you if you cry. All my mates would take the piss if they knew. Not my missus – she accepted me for the way I was,' Jack said.

It was clear that talking to Angelica felt lovely because it was the antithesis of stress. Angelica created a safe haven so Jack could confide his most personal feelings to her, without fearing judgement.

'I told her things I would never tell anyone else. Only her,' said Jack.

Now I could see Jack's mince pies filling up. They looked like half-filled snow globes. If it was Christmas and they could be shaken, I knew what he would wish for: he would wish he could talk to his wife.

Angelica had died a year ago.

Maybe it's more accurate to say therapy is the listening cure, rather than the talking cure. Now, in therapy, Jack needed me to listen to how much he missed Angelica. He had come to therapy to confide his pain.

Angelica had been Jack's first and only confidant. Tiramisu was also not their only food ritual – Jack once said he always made sure he gave Angelica his first Rolo, as well as his last. It was a sweet story which clearly told me that in Jack's personal hierarchy of attachment figures, Angelica came first and foremost. Jack had lots of mates he would go to the pub or play golf with, but he had only really talked to his wife. He had put all his eggs in one basket.

This was a problem I was familiar with from my research. I am really fortunate to have collaborated with some of Bowlby's colleagues, and over the years we have continued the legacy of his work about the impact of stressful life events. Our research has consistently shown that if you have at least two close, confiding relationships with people who give you emotional support, then you are more likely to be securely attached. Having Angelica alone as his confidant left Jack vulnerable to insecurity. Her death had pushed him into a position where he needed to seek out other people to talk to – and this started with me.

Over the course of our work, Jack learned to confide in someone new. As the therapy moved forwards, Jack started to share his feelings and slowly revealed himself in a way that allowed me to truly know him.

One day, Jack unconsciously shared a little more than he intended to. He was telling me a story about Angelica during her last days, when his stomach let out a loud gurgling noise.

'Oops. My belly is joining in the conversation,' said Jack, leaning back into his chair. He smiled softly at me. If I had to describe that smile, I would use the Greek word *charmolypi*, which means 'joyful sorrow'.

There was something cathartic happening right now. Jack didn't need to confide how he felt. I could hear it. The tummy gurgle was a response from his rest-and-digest system. His body was telling us that he didn't feel stressed. Jack was feeling at ease enough to digest both his food and the difficult feelings we had talked about. Perhaps therapy, and I, had started to feel like his safe haven.

A year or so into Jack's therapy, the British snack brand McVitie's started their Let's Talk campaign to promote the importance of conversation and connection for mental health. They encouraged people to 'be kind to your mind' by sitting down and having a proper chat with someone over a cuppa and a biscuit. I think we can safely say that Jack and Angelica got there first with tiramisu.

And, of course, Rosie Lee.

(That means tea.)

* * *

Tea-ramisu

This isn't Angelica's classic tiramisu, but it's my homage to her and Jack's ti/tea for two ritual. Eat this when you are resting and digesting with your nearest and dearest confidant.

Serves 2

1 English breakfast tea bag
1 large egg
50g caster sugar
4 tablespoons spiced rum (or you could be traditional
   and use Marsala)

75g mascarpone
50ml double cream
12 savoiardi biscuits (Italian sponge fingers)
Ground cinnamon, for dusting

Make a small, strong cup of black tea with the tea bag. Leave aside to cool.

Separate the egg yolk from the white, putting them in two separate large bowls. Whisk the egg yolk with half the sugar and half the rum until pale and airy. In another bowl, soften the mascarpone by whisking it, making sure it's smooth. Then stir it into the yolk mixture.

In another bowl, whip the cream until you have soft peaks, then set aside. Whisk the egg white with the remaining sugar until you have stiff peaks.

Gently fold the whipped cream into the yolk mixture, followed by the whisked egg white, until completely combined.

Stir the remaining rum into the tea and pour it into a shallow bowl. Time to assemble the tea-ramisus – you will need two small bowls (or large teacups). Dip the biscuits briefly into the tea mixture. Put three soaked biscuits into the bottom of each bowl and top with the cream mixture. Repeat this layering once more. Refrigerate until you are ready to eat. Dust the surface of each tea-ramisu with cinnamon before serving.

5

A Twice-Told Recipe

*Can you change your recipe for relationships
and get a better result?*

One of my favourite food writers, Laurie Colwin, said, 'When people enter the kitchen, they often drag their childhoods with them.'

When people enter relationships, they do the same thing. The reason this happens is because of recipes, and by that I mean the unconscious, psychological sort. These find their way into all relationships, including the therapy relationship. But sometimes the culinary kind come into relationships too. With my patient Aisling, both types of recipe entered the therapy.

Aisling was a food photographer and a recipe developer. She was 24 years old, and since finishing her degree, Aisling had spent the last few years honing her craft in several internships, including one at the BBC. She was becoming increasingly discouraged by not being able to secure a full-time job. I could see this as she dragged her feet into our session every week. Aisling always wore white frill ankle socks that reminded me of doilies. I assumed she wore the socks because they were pretty, and not because they were a throwback to 1980s cake photography, which she was too young to have witnessed.

Aisling had an eye for detail, not only for the food in her photos, but also in her appearance. Hanging on her charm bracelet were mini versions of most of the utensils and equipment I had in my kitchen, including a tiny candy-apple-red KitchenAid, the cutest jewellery item I've ever seen. She exceeded her five-a-day in accessories alone. As our work went on, I saw dangly cherry earrings, a pineapple pendant, avocado studs, a headband with lemons and oranges and a strawberry-shaped basket bag. The short nails on her hands stood out because they were painted in bright primary colours. Shades of red and yellow seemed to be Aisling's favourites, so the ends of her fingers often looked like very juicy pomegranate seeds or large kernels of sweetcorn.

Aisling said that she had always wanted to be a food photographer; she didn't feel the same way about travel photography, nature photography or portrait photography. She had a pronounced disdain for wedding photography, which I found interesting. Aisling said, 'Well, my mum isn't a hopeless romantic or a daydreamer. Neither is my dad. So it seems only logical for me not to be either. They aren't the most picturesque version of love and life.'

It was psychological, not logical, and it was part of Aisling's recipe for relationships. She had learned, step by step, from her parents' marriage that romantic relationships were hopeless, and a drag.

Aisling's other recipes – the food ones – and their accompanying photos, entered the therapy quite quickly. In her case, it was the word recipe in its truest form, which is Latin, and means 'to take' – one person gives and another receives. Aisling would bring her recipes in and physically hand them to me to see. She had first made recipe cards for her undergraduate final year project, but had enjoyed making them so much that she continued doing so after she finished university. Every now and then when she created a new one, she would bring it in to show me. When I first saw some of Aisling's recipe cards, I was taken by surprise. I mean, I was so surprised that for a second I thought she was showing me recipe cards from Waitrose. They were that good. In fact, Aisling's recipe cards knocked the socks off Waitrose's. It was the most picturesque food I had ever seen.

Her recipes were just as creative, and seemed delicious. The triple chocolate coconut meringues were my favourite: milk and dark and white chocolate swirled into big, bounteous meringues. I imagined they tasted like a Bounty bar. Aisling had photographed them from directly above, on cool slate grey tiles, and she had rained desiccated coconut and teeny tiny chocolate curls over the whole lot. It was like something out of a more sophisticated, grown-up Willy Wonka chocolate factory, and all of that swirling chocolate was magical, almost hypnotic, as though the

meringues were saying 'you know you want to eat me'.
I noticed that in Aisling's card collection the recipes were
mostly for desserts, which was curious. After all, no one
needs a dessert, so I always feel that desserts say something
about desire.

The recipe cards were a little like show and tell at school.
The interactions were sweet; I felt a bit like Miss Honey
in *Matilda*, which wasn't surprising given how talented
I thought Aisling was. After the showing of the card came
the telling of the story behind it. And then, at the end of the
session, Aisling would always leave the recipe card behind
on the coffee table, saying that I could keep it if I wanted
to. I did want to, and I sensed that Aisling wanted to know
that I wanted to. So as you can see, our relationship came
into the therapy room quite quickly too, in terms of this
giving and receiving recipe ritual. I soon realised that the
card-giving was really caregiving, and an expression of
Aisling's attachment needs. It told me something about her
early relational life, which Aisling was very willing to talk
about. Aisling didn't drag her childhood into our conversations; she brought it in reflectively from our very first
session. She said, 'My mum's experiences have probably
helped to shape me into who I am, and I think that's poten-
tially one of the biggest things I can unpack here with you.
I haven't woken up this fully formed person.'

As we worked together, Aisling told me some things
about her food life that had been formative. In one session,
she said: 'Growing up, I was told you were to only have

one hot meal a day – something my mum was taught by her mum. I've never known a time when my mum wasn't counting calories religiously. She taught me to only butter one side of bread when making a sandwich to save calories, and we never drank full-fat milk. She would weigh herself every day. For a short period of time when I was a child, they thought I was lactose intolerant. So my mum had to keep a very close eye on my food and I had to be weighed every day, which I think only fed into my mum's own obsession. I suppose eating disorders and food photography have two things in common – an obsession with food.'

While Aisling never described herself as explicitly having an eating disorder, she said that her 'eating became disordered' during the early part of her adolescence. She talked about using all the same 'tricks' her mother had used, and also some just for her, such as skipping lunch at school (the sandwich with butter only on one side went in the bin), cutting her hot meal at dinner time into smaller-than-bitesize pieces and putting them into her napkin when no one was watching, and 'not doing a number two' before being weighed.

These were all things I had heard before.

Many years ago, as part of my research, I worked at a residential treatment centre for young people with eating disorders. At the time, there were ten girls staying there. Most were teenagers, and the youngest was just ten years old. All were in the throes of severe anorexia. It wasn't an unusual sight to see the patients walking around with nasogastric tubes, and some were so weak they couldn't climb the stairs to their bedrooms, so they had to take the stair lift. It was hard to get used to seeing that. I don't think I ever really did.

My role was to do attachment interviews. I was struck by how, just like Aisling, all of the patients had a lot of insight into what was 'disordered' in their lives – and it wasn't only food. As one fourteen-year-old patient said to me, 'I think my family are the reason I got ill really. Well, not them, but the dynamics of my family.' This was the thing that came up most often in conversations with other members of staff at the centre, from the psychiatrists to the psychoanalysts to the nurses, even the dieticians and chefs: the fact that eating disorders are hardly ever about food. The symptoms are really about something else. According to attachment theory, that something else is relationship experiences – those dynamics of what goes on with our loved ones. So mental health has relational roots, not just surface symptoms. In my own work with the patients, I heard story after story about attachments that were insecure and inverted; the daughters were often pulled into the role of parenting their parents and had no one to seek support from or to connect with. Aisling told me a similar tale. She said when she found her best friends, Olive and Ophelia, at secondary school, her symptoms 'miraculously disappeared'. Still, Aisling described the leftover feeling since then as 'never-ending grief'. Those connections with her friends had shone a light on what she hadn't had at home.

Aisling's home life was one of caregiving; her mother was disabled and her health – both physically and psychologically – had been on a downward spiral since the stroke she'd had when Aisling was thirteen. Shortly after that, Aisling found herself taking photos of food. She said, 'I saw a disposable camera in a shop, and I bought it. I don't really know why but I started taking photos of the food in my mum's *Delicious* and *BBC Good Food* magazines. I liked any food with hands in the frame, or dinner-table scenes. It was like I wanted to remember what human, family food was like. I couldn't really cook, but I had to all the time after mum had her stroke.'

Aisling still prepared her mother's breakfast, lunch and dinner, fed her, bathed her, dressed her and put her to bed every night. In our sessions, I often had to remind myself that we were talking about Aisling's mother, not Aisling's daughter. Her mother wasn't her secure base. Aisling could never leave her, even for a short time, to go off and explore the world, as she was always worried something was going to happen to her. Aisling had no opportunity for a life of her own. There was no time to hang out with Olive and Ophelia, and she'd never had a boyfriend ('What's the point?' was Aisling's opinion about that).

Aisling's mother had no other support – or, more precisely, she didn't see the point in any other support when she had her daughter to care for her. She was especially critical of Aisling's father. He couldn't cook, nor could he look after the house, himself or anyone else. Aisling said,

'My dad has clung to me like a life raft, desperate to keep afloat, not to get lost in his sea of depression. I love my family, but sometimes it feels like we're three people just bound together by sadness.'

Since childhood, Aisling had been lost at sea, with neither a secure base nor a safe haven. So she'd learned to be creative with her attachment needs by caring for those who were supposed to care for her. When care-seeking isn't on the cards, then caregiving is a good alternative, because you at least gain some closeness with, and availability from, your attachment figures. These dynamics didn't allow for any attachment security within Aisling's family. It also sounded to me as though Aisling was the glue that bound her parents together. She was their only child, and they didn't have much of a relationship without her. There hadn't been much love between them even before Aisling was born.

'My mum has told me time and time again that she doesn't want me to get married or to have kids because then this surely means I'll end up just like her, which is dependent on a man,' said Aisling. It seemed Aisling's mother wasn't unconsciously passing down a recipe for relationships to Aisling; she was forcing it down her throat. 'My mum has often said that she watched her friends around her settle down so she felt like my dad was the last resort. Sometimes I could imagine nothing worse than being like my mother: sixty-five, disabled, dependent on a man who unfortunately you're stuck with because you were desperate enough to settle. I don't know how I feel about marriage and children – just growing up with my parents is enough to put me off for life.'

Aisling was firing like a camera in burst mode the day she said that.

In the following session, she softened a little around the edges.

'I remember I read this poem once, I can't remember who wrote it, but it said that love is a dirty thing to want. I feel like that's what I've learned from my mum,' she said.

Aisling's recipe for relationships couldn't have been more different to her heartful, beautiful and glossy recipe cards. Love is dirty. Don't be dependent. Don't need, let alone want, anything or anyone.

Your recipe for relationships, as I like to call it, is one of the most important concepts in attachment theory. Bowlby used a more technical term and called it the internal working model. It is what it says on the box: it's internal, so it's invisible and unconscious; it's working, so it's on all the time; and it's a model, so it's built based on your past relationship experiences, and includes feelings, memories, wishes, intentions and expectations. Because your model, or your recipe, is being built right from the beginning, from when you are held and fed in that first relationship, it has a long hold on you. That's why you drag it with you into the present, even though you don't mean to. And when you do drag it in, because the recipe is based on past ingredients, it inevitably reflects the past, not the present.

It's also a twice-told recipe: it tells you how you feel about yourself, and how you feel about others, particularly your attachment figures.

Do you know Philip Larkin's poem 'This Be The Verse'? It's the one with the infamous lines: 'They fuck you up, your mum and dad / They may not mean to, but they do'. I don't know how well Larkin knew attachment theory, but he's basically talking about the internal working model. Actually, the next lines of the poem: 'They fill you with the faults they had / And add some extra, just for you' are also related to what we're talking about. The technical term for that in attachment theory is intergenerational transmission. Attachment is 'transmitted' from one generation to the next, and this happens through relationship recipes. But even when a recipe (psychological or food) is passed down from your parent, it doesn't keep its original form – it's you who adds the extras. You build your own model based on how you see things internally, in your mind's eye – and that might not match with things externally. Although Aisling had seen her mother being dependent, she didn't have that trait – and never had. According to her family, Aisling had even 'potty trained herself'. From the word go, Aisling had created her own recipe, which was 'don't depend'. As she also said to me, 'Maybe my mum hasn't had to make love a dirty thing – I've already done that myself.'

In the last twenty years, some attachment researchers have refined the internal working model to make it even more recipe-like, with what's called secure base scripts. This is how your internal working model talks to you and tells you what to do. Just like a recipe, your script includes ingredients and a method that guides you to the set goal, such as: 'My loved one is there for me. They are a loving person. I am loved. When I am stressed, I can seek them out for support. This will comfort me and help me to deal with the stress.' That's the secure version. There will obviously be different versions for all of the different attachment styles. Those F-words I mentioned earlier on are the external manifestation of your internal working model. When a model, script or recipe comes into therapy, the technical word for that is transference. It's unconscious, but it's a necessary part of the process, because the patient and the therapist can test the recipe 'live' and explore it in the here and now of the therapy, seeing what works and what doesn't and why. This provides the opportunity to rework the recipe. Bowlby believed that was the task of therapy.

After the first year, fewer of Aisling's recipes entered the therapy – the culinary ones, that is. And when they did come in, I noticed they were very different from the previous ones. There was also a theme – dark brown – and not in an inviting, cup-of-cocoa kind of way. One recipe card was for lamb stew (the photograph showed four huge lumps of meat sitting in a murky gravy). Another card was for chocolate mousse (that was just dumped into a big bowl). A further one was for chocolate truffles (I can't polish my comment for that one: they looked like turds). Aisling didn't offer to let me keep those cards. When I pointed out this difference compared to the previous cards, Aisling replied using the same phrase each time: 'They're shit'. I wondered if she was really saying, or showing me, 'I'm shit'. She was still struggling to find work and had received rejection after rejection. In most of our sessions she would cry.

'Look, they look like shit. The lighting is all wrong. I look like I've pulled those photos out of my arse. They're repugnant – a complete shit show,' said Aisling, as she sobbed, 'I can't even get work in food without my photos. No one even wants to see my recipes.'

She was almost wailing in pain as she wished she could claw herself out of 'this dark hole' she was lost in. Something was certainly opening up or being moved within Aisling. She was becoming alive to her recipe, the part that was about her relationship with herself, and how unseen and unloved she felt. Aisling was slowly being pulled into a place that, emotionally, felt as dark and deadened and dismal as the food in those brown photos.

***

It was once said that a good therapist fights darkness and seeks illumination. During that time with Aisling, however, I couldn't quite see how I was going to do that. The therapy was starting to feel stuck. I mean, really stuck. But if there was a person who knew how, it was the man who said those words: the American therapist Irvin Yalom.

That darkness and illumination stuff is from his most well-known book, *Love's Executioner*. But that's not the book I'm going to tell you about now.

In another of his books, *Existential Psychotherapy*, Yalom opens by telling the reader about an Armenian cooking class he attended with his friends. For him, this cooking class was a moment of illumination.

In the Armenian cooking class, Yalom and his friends watched the teacher prepare an array of amazing aubergine and lamb dishes. Since she couldn't speak English and they couldn't speak Armenian, she taught by demonstration and they observed her. They kept a keen watch in the kitchen and tried as hard as they could to cook the recipes. But try as they might, they couldn't duplicate her dishes.

Sometimes things do go wrong in the kitchen. I remember Julia Child once talked about how the mousse refuses to leave the mould or the potatoes stick to the skillet or the apple charlotte slowly collapses. She also wrote in one of her books, 'If you're alone in the kitchen and you drop the lamb, you can always just pick it up. Who's going to know?'

Anyway, Yalom didn't drop his lamb during that class. But one day, after wondering for so long what gave his teacher's cooking that special touch, the answer fell on him. He noticed his teacher go off-*reci*piste (I just made that up now) and throw in handful after handful of assorted spices and condiments during the preparation of one of the dishes. Yalom was convinced it was these 'throw-ins', these added ingredients that were not part of the original recipe, that made all the difference. Yalom believes the same thing happens in therapy: the therapist throws in an added extra, the 'real thing', when no one is looking. Or, as Julia Child said, you pick up the lamb.

Yalom says throw-ins have been coming into therapy since the start, and in his book, after he talks about the Armenian cooking class, he details some of them. Freud's throw-ins included telling one of his patients to visit her sister's grave and, on another occasion, to drop by to see a man she fancied. I remember reading a story once about Ainsworth's therapist, whose exact words to her in their first session were: 'First, get some new clothes, the right length, and for God's sake, something with some colour. And secondly, do something about your hair.' (It's worth saying that Ainsworth took great pleasure in shopping and getting her hair done in the following days. When Ainsworth arrived for her second session, the first thing her analyst said to her was 'Much better!' She was delighted.)

Yalom talks about having a 'huge grab-bag' of therapeutic approaches, which I guess is where he keeps all his added extras. There is, in fact, an entire book about Yalom's biggest throw-in with a patient. That book is called *Every Day Gets a Little Closer* and it's about his work with Ginny, who was an aspiring novelist in the middle of severe writer's block. To help with her inertia, Yalom asked Ginny to write an honest summary of their session every week, and to add in any thoughts, feelings, expectations, interpretations and associations that hadn't consciously come into the room. He did the same, and in the hope of therapeutic benefit, they exchanged notes every six months. Yalom said he couldn't predict the exact effects of the exercise, but felt sure it would stir up something powerful. And it did. After working together for two years in therapy, their reflections were published side by side in the book. That's why it's subtitled *A Twice-Told Therapy*.

Unlike Yalom, I don't have a huge grab-bag of techniques; mine is more like a small lunch box with a few foodie tactics packed into it. Still, one day, about two years into the therapy with Aisling, I found myself reaching into it and pulling something out and throwing it into the therapy. At the time, because Aisling had even stopped creating brown photos and recipes, I thought my idea was worth a try. I hoped it might bring some light into the darkness.

On that day, at the start of our session, Aisling asked me how I was, as she did every week. My usual reply when patients ask me this question is: 'I'm fine, thank you for asking'.

But that day I said: 'Actually, Aisling, I've been holding you in mind and I wanted to mention something to you. I'm writing a book about food, love and relationships. It's more of a story-telling book than a cookery book, but there are recipes in it, and I was wondering how you felt about me possibly including one of yours?'

Aisling was quiet. Her head tilted slightly and she raised her eyebrows. She looked at me as if I had just asked her something in Armenian. I felt like I had just dropped the lamb in the kitchen. But I wasn't alone. Because Aisling was there and still looking right at me.

She didn't say a word. She just held my eyes intently.

There I was, feeling like I had given Aisling's chocolate mousse photo a run for its money, when, after about a minute, she asked me a question that I wasn't expecting.

'You've kept them?' said Aisling, softly.

It told me everything I needed to know about her expectations of others.

'Yes. I've put all your recipe cards into a folder, which I keep in my kitchen. I made the chocolate meringues the other day,' I said.

'Really?' she said. Her head shook a little, and so did the cherries on her ears. 'I had to remake them two separate times for that card because the melted chocolate was too hot for the stiff peaks on the meringue. I cried a lot, more out of frustration than anything else.'

'I agree, it was tricky swirling all the chocolate, but fun too. I enjoyed following your recipe, and eating them even more. They were delicious,' I said.

We had a small silence. Aisling tapped her pomegranated finger nails on the arm of her chair.

'Is it okay if I take some time to think about it?' said Aisling.

'Of course,' I said.

I was worried I'd messed up. After the session, my own script every day for the rest of that week was: you're not Yalom, you know.

***

When Aisling returned for our session the following week, she said she didn't want me to use one of her recipe card recipes. I said that was perfectly fine (because it was) and that I was glad she felt able to say so.

Then Aisling said she wanted me to use a new recipe.

'I spent a really long time thinking and I decided I wanted to give you a recipe that's the most meaningful to me. I settled on fairy cakes. I've never created a card for it because I've always thought it was too basic and so it would have little value,' she said. 'So there's no photo, but there's a memory of my mum and a story I can tell you.'

Aisling had brought her two recipes together, and into the room with her.

It was now time for mine to enter.

'Aisling, I think that fairy cakes are a great idea. Thank you for giving it so much thought. But I have also been thinking about how it felt for you that I asked you for something. I was wondering whether it put pressure on you to take care of me, like you do in your relationship with your mother. Given your experience, it's understandable that you might expect the same from me,' I said, putting all of our recipes straight on the table for discussion.

Aisling met me there. She opened her handbag and took out a slightly weathered polaroid photo, leaned across the coffee table and handed it to me. It was a photo of Aisling as a little girl and her mother in the kitchen. Aisling couldn't have been older than four. She was chubby-cheeked and dressed in a pair of denim dungarees embellished with strawberries. Aisling's mother had short curly hair. They both had bright eyes and big 'say cheese!' toothy smiles.

'It's obviously not a food photo of fairy cakes, or one that I took. My mum took it. An old-school selfie,' said Aisling.

What a photo. It was a moment in time where nothing else mattered.

'Sometimes I think the only thing I've learned from my parents' relationship is not to have a relationship like that. I don't know how well my mum ever got on with my dad, probably not well enough from how things have worked out. My mum is obviously the way she is through her own experiences – not only her health, but her family. She grew up surrounded by women. She went to an all-girls' Catholic school and only had friends who were girls. She brought up her four sisters and never had anyone to take care of her. My experience is awfully similar because I've taken care of her,' said Aisling. 'But my mum was the one to encourage my creativity, she cared about it – and that's what it felt like when you asked. My mum was in and out of hospital for most of my time at uni, so she wasn't part of it. She never really saw any of my work. She couldn't come to my graduation. It wasn't always that way. In this photo, we're happy – blindingly so. Photos don't let you forget. Love wasn't always sad or dirty.'

Then Aisling told me more about her chosen recipe, which her mother had seen and been part of. She said, 'I was thinking about the first thing I cried about here with you; it was the fact that my mum rarely cooked when I was growing up because her disability meant she couldn't stand up for long enough to make anything. Sometimes I would ask to bake fairy cakes, probably like most kids. It was the only thing we ever baked. We made them together. She would sit at the kitchen table and read out the recipe and I would stand at the counter and put the ingredients into her ancient yellow Kenwood mixer. She had photocopied a page out of a children's recipe book from the library; she used to take me to Rhyme Time there when I was little. She kept the recipe in her little calorie-counting diary. I found it but the words had rubbed out completely after twenty years, so it isn't much use. I think it's like a normal fairy cake recipe – you know, equal quantities of flour, sugar, butter and eggs.'

The recipe for fairy cakes was familiar to me; in fact, I knew it well. As for Aisling's relationship recipe, the same one hadn't entered the room. It was mix of past and present, and of different attachment figures, and it included an interaction from our relationship: the first time she had been vulnerable with me.

After a moment of quiet, Aisling asked me something else I wasn't expecting:

'I don't know if my memory of the recipe is right. I'm not sure if you have a childhood one too. I thought if you did, we could use that for fairy cakes?'

Aisling had asked me for something. It was an 'I want' or, more specifically, 'I desire this dessert', with an added,

'And this is how I want it'. Perhaps you might say she had asked me for care. Maybe it was a moment of dependency.

Whatever it was, it was a first.

We had started to rework Aisling's recipe.

***

Postscript

I have more than twice told this story. I've talked about it in both my own therapy and in clinical supervision. The short, 'This Be The Verse'-inspired version of the script that came out was: I fuck it up, I don't mean to but I do. As you can see, this experience with Aisling unexpectedly threw a lot of light on parts of my own recipe. For that whole week, I was worried that I had fucked up the therapy. Now, on reflection, I don't think I fucked it up. What I did was take a risk, which is definitely different for my relationship recipe. So I guess something has been reworked along the way.

I'm not Yalom (that part of my script has stayed) but this chapter has ended up having more in common with *A Twice-Told Therapy* than I expected. What started off as an add-in ended up being all-in; both Aisling's recipe and full story have been included, and the process of this chapter has been different to the others: we have told the story together. I had initially planned to include the recipe for fairy cakes in another chapter, in more of an anonymised way, but many months later, after I started to write the book and as it took shape, it didn't feel true to do that. It felt right to honour Aisling's most meaningful recipe with more of her own relationship recipe. I found myself wanting to write about therapeutic change, and I thought that shining a spotlight on our interaction in therapy around the fairy cake recipe would do that well. So I took another risk and asked Aisling how she felt about the idea. She liked it, and said, 'You'll find more creativity with that.' I think she was right.

Then she added: 'My relationship with my mum has definitely moulded me into who I am. Maybe you'll get to tell that story in your book.'

So I did. Or, we did. That has been the story we've told here.

After I wrote a draft of the chapter, I showed Aisling and invited her to comment, and we took care together to anonymise some of the identifying details without distorting her story or our story. So Aisling had the opportunity to see parts of me and my process and my recipe for relationships. As Yalom said of his experience with Ginny, it was an exercise in self-disclosure, and a powerful one at that. I am reminded again of what the word recipe means: one person gives and another receives. In our work, both writing and in therapy, Aisling got to receive me, to see me as more human. I am not infallible, omniscient, untroubled or perfectly put-together. I am still figuring my shit out (which reminds me: the truffle turd comment is Aisling's, but we polished those words together).

89

The throw-in wasn't pulled out of the sky (or my arse, as Aisling would say): it was grounded in attachment theory and the psychological reality that our relationship experiences make us who we are. In the same way Yalom saw Ginny as a gifted writer, I saw Aisling as being gifted with food. In our first session she had said she was 'completely desperate' to be a food photographer and a recipe developer, a comment which I found curious. In my mind, she always was a food photographer and a recipe developer, and I had thought this since she shared her first recipe card with me. I wanted to help her, or perhaps you could say, take care of her. By asking Aisling for a recipe, I wanted to show her that she was seen. It's something every human being needs. But I have also found that patients in particular need to know you see them *as something*. And when you see someone as something *they* want to be, rather than who *you* want them to be, it's a really powerful relational process; it says you've listened and held them in mind and imagined them. I know how much that has meant to me in my own therapy. It's one of the ways that therapy can give you a new relationship experience, and that's what I wanted to give Aisling.

In all the years that I've taught and researched attachment theory, there is one question that comes up the most often: Can you change your attachment style? In other words, can you rework your recipe? In line with what I have seen and learned along the way, my answer is yes. Attachment theory understands things backwards, but at its heart, it is a forward-looking and hopeful theory. An internal working model isn't destiny. It's working, not worked. To change it, it means working on what can be worked on. What I mean is that you can't change the past and you can't change other people. Learning to live with the things that can't be changed can actually be a change in itself for some people. Don't get me wrong: all of this reworking stuff isn't easy. Going through and exploring all of the ingredients in your recipe, deciding whether they still have a place, is often a painful and slow process. But with support from a 'trusted companion', as Bowlby said, you can update and correct and, over time, build a new model that works better for you.

After telling people about mishaps of the lamb, the potatoes and the apple charlotte, Julia Child went on to say: 'One of the secrets of cooking is to learn to correct something if you can, and bear with it if you cannot.'

That's also the secret of therapy.

As I write this, Aisling's therapy remains ongoing. She is bearing with being human (I am too). She still isn't 'this fully formed person' (neither am I). But we're working on it. And every session we get a little closer.

* * *

Fairy Cakes

My recipe and Aisling's recipe, told together.

Makes 12

For the cakes:

100g caster sugar
100g margarine or room-temperature butter
100g self-raising flour
2 teaspoons baking powder
2 eggs
1 teaspoon vanilla extract

For the icing:
100g icing sugar
4 teaspoons water
Decorations, such as silver balls, jelly diamonds and
hundreds and thousands

Preheat the oven to 190°C/170°C fan/gas mark 5 and line
a 12-cup muffin tray with fairy cake cases.

Put all of the cake ingredients into a big bowl and mix
by hand with a wooden spoon (Andrea). Or put the cake
ingredients into the bowl of a stand mixer or a food processor and mix (Aisling). Stop mixing when everything is
combined and the batter is smooth.

Place two teaspoons of cake batter into each fairy
cake case.

Pop the muffin tray in the oven and bake the cakes for
15 minutes, or until they are risen and golden. Remove

the tray from the oven and let it stand for 5 minutes.
Take the cakes out of the tray and place onto a wire rack
to cool.

To make the icing, sieve the icing sugar into a bowl, add
the water and stir well until the mixture drops easily off a
spoon; if it's too thick, add a little more water, a teaspoon-
ful at a time. Smooth a spoonful of icing over each cake.
Before the icing sets, decorate each fairy cake with your
choice of sprinkles.

Part II

SEPARATION

6

Flying the
(Shredded Wheat) Nest

*Why don't boundaries need to be barriers
in your relationships?*

This story is about my Big Fat Greek therapy experience. At least, the beginnings of it. It was big and fat figuratively, in that I had some big, food-related feelings about the therapy that filled me up a lot. And it was Greek because that's what I am. So was my patient, Artemis: Greek goddess of the hunt.

'I've heard good things about you, Dr Andrea,' Artemis said in our first session.

'From who?' I'm not a fan of being pedestalled, but I was curious so I asked.

'It was Maria Charalambous. Her husband's cousin, Katerina, knows you from Middlesex University,' said Artemis.

'I see.' I nodded in acknowledgement. I had no idea who this person was.

'I saw you've done some research on hormones, no? And eating disorders too? This is why I think you can help Electra.' Now Artemis was the one who was nodding, as though she was trying to convince herself of something.

'Electra?' I said.

'Electra is my daughter. *Psyche mou*,' Artemis said, with an almost 'coochy coo' sentimentality. In Greek, *psyche mou* means 'my soul'. Electra was seventeen years old and Artemis' life and soul, the apple of her eye. Electra was also, seemingly, broken. 'I need you to help me fix Electra,' Artemis announced, as she went on to list all the reasons why Electra needed fixing. The main one involved food.

'She doesn't eat enough. I've told her she must stay at home for university so that I can cook for her. I'm worried she has some kind of eating disorder, Dr Andrea. She is skinny and she's tall too. Just like you.' I wasn't sure if that was a dig or a compliment. Sometimes comments about physical appearance can be a way of getting closer to someone. Artemis was certainly close to home. She was old enough to be my mother, and she was also my first Greek patient. Artemis looked like a bigger, very well-fed version of Nana Mouskouri, the famous Greek singer. She had rich black-brown, shoulder-length hair and square spectacles with thick black rims. Her voice was theatrical (Greek tragedy) and she conducted it with her big waving hands. I imagined the love she gave to Electra was heavy-handed and old-fashioned – a give-with-one-hand-yank-back-with-the-other sort of love that came straight out the 1950s Greek Cypriot village.

'I love her. I cook for her every day but she don't want none of it. And I do all good, healthy food, you know. *Dolmades, keftedes, kleftiko, stifado, afelia, moussaka.* You know, what your mama must cook for you,' said Artemis, as she leaned slightly forward and smiled at me. I found myself backing into my chair as far as I possibly could. I wasn't sure if Artemis was actually asking me a question but I backed out of answering that too. I held the smiling silence and said nothing. Self-disclosure in therapy is a controversial issue in any case, but now, in session one with Artemis, was not the time to reveal that my own maternal cooking legacy was more Iceland than motherland. My mother's secret ingredient when she makes moussaka? Birds Eye potato waffles.

Artemis then turned up the wattage on her smile. 'Dr Andrea, you have a beautiful website!'

'Thank you, Artemis, that's kind,' I said, slightly worried that she'd short-circuit after hearing the next bit: 'I do want to hear more from you about what's bringing you here to therapy, but I need to let you know that it's impossible for me to fix or change Electra. That's not how therapy works. But what we can do is help you to understand your relationship with Electra and why it is distressing for you. It's important that with our time today I tell you about how we would work together.'

'Yes, okay. Fine,' said Artemis. I detected her disappointment, which left me feeling like a mother who had told her child they couldn't have sweets before supper. By the end of that first session, I think I had fallen off my pedestal.

***

A week later, at the same time of 10.30 a.m., I was due to see Artemis for our second session. At 10.39 a.m. I received a text from her:

> Hello Dr Andrea, forgive me, I am running late. I am just picking up a coffee on the way, would you like me to get you one too? With sugar? *Metrio* or *glyko*?

Artemis was asking how much sugar I wanted: one spoonful or two. There was something sweetly naïve about her coffee offer, and it was clear that today I needed to go over what's known as the therapeutic frame, the invisible boundary that 'holds' the therapy and sets out where, when and how the work is going to happen. Otherwise this therapy was going to become coffee time at the village *kafeneio*.

In the meantime, I had to respond to Artemis in a way that held her as my patient.

> Dear Artemis, thank you for the coffee offer but I am fine. I will look forward to seeing you soon for our session.

Artemis arrived ten minutes later with an espresso-sized takeaway coffee cup in one hand and a hessian shopping bag in the other. She was also carrying a canvas tote bag on one shoulder and a leather messenger bag on the other. Artemis sat down and arranged her bags carefully around her feet, like they were presents at the bottom of a Christmas tree. When she finished, she looked up at me, like I was the fairy at the top of the tree. I took that as my cue to start the session.

'Artemis, I think it's important to take some time today to explain how we will work together, if we are to proceed with therapy. This includes things like the time and duration of our sessions, where our sessions will take place, payment information and what happens if you miss or cancel a session, and also privacy and confidentiality. It's necessary that we both agree on this. I've got the information here for you in writing, I do this for clarity because it helps us both to know where we stand,' I said, pointing at the contract I'd printed out and put on the table, which Artemis had placed her coffee cup next to.

'Of course. I am listening,' Artemis said, as she bent down and opened up the hessian bag. She took out a large cube-shaped cool bag, unzipped it and removed a small square plastic container from inside. She said, 'I hope you don't mind if I eat while we talk? I have a long meeting this afternoon and I won't have time for lunch.' There was a whiff of panic in her voice, like she was anxious about the hunger monster striking later. In any case, it was a rhetorical question. As Artemis opened the box, a fishy odour spread through the room: a mound of pale pink taramasalata filled the pot. She click-clacked open another rectangular plastic container; it was like the vegetable stall of a food market, with rows of rainbow-coloured crudités including carrot, cucumber and celery batons, canoe-shaped slices of red, yellow and green bell peppers, cauliflower florets and mini radishes. Then she unfolded a foil pouch that had triangles of pitta. Artemis felt like a conjuror with a magical meze bag; whoosh, out came another dish. Olives were next (both black kalamata and cracked green olives with lemon and coriander seeds) and finally, cubes of feta.

We were way past *kafeneio*. We were in a taverna.

'This is my taramasalata. Homemade. Electra didn't eat any last night. She never eats my cooking anymore. She has always been a picky eater. Always. Since she was a little girl, we would take her for meze and she never put nothing on her plate.' Artemis looked a little perturbed as she used the pitta as a shovel to eat the taramasalata. Her last comment was curious. Picky eating is not necessarily non-compliant behaviour, it's actually attachment behaviour about boundaries. Through food that is either allowed in or kept out, what the child is really trying to do is explore and express what makes them feel safe.

Artemis ate almost as quickly as she talked. She was certainly expressive. There was no censoring or editing or bowdlerising, no filters or breaks or pauses, or any time at all for inhaling and exhaling air. Apart from the eating, it was a textbook example of what Freud called free association, which is when a patient says whatever is going through their mind. As I listened, I noticed that her pitta-shovelling sped up when she spoke about 'losing Electra'; it was as though she was trying to fill a void with food. I also noticed that the written agreement was now serving as a tablecloth for the meze. After Artemis had eaten her lunch and cleared away the plastic containers, we went through the document. Artemis was quiet as we did so; she didn't ask any questions. I wondered if she had some feelings about me explicitly setting out the boundaries of our work, but she expressly said no when I asked. Then Artemis asserted her own boundary and ended our session at 11.17 a.m., a few minutes early, saying she needed to get to work. She folded up the contract into a triangle like the pitta and tucked it into her handbag. As Artemis gathered the rest of her bags, she confirmed that she would like to continue with therapy. After she left, I spotted an olive stone underneath her chair. I found myself thinking that I probably should have written something specific about food in our agreement, but it was a bit late for that now.

***

Artemis arrived late again for our third session. She sat down without taking her bags off her shoulders and started to tell me about the 'drama' with Electra that had happened the previous night. Artemis had gone into Electra's room to 'tell her' that she must stay in and study for the whole weekend and that she could not see her boyfriend for the next month, until her exams were over. Electra protested but Artemis said she didn't care and that she must do as she was told. A little while later, Artemis called Electra for dinner, but Electra told her she wasn't hungry. Artemis decided to take Electra's dinner to her bedroom. She walked straight into Electra's room with the tray of food without knocking first. It appeared that Electra had a three strikes rule, and that was strike one: physical boundary violation. Electra repeatedly said she wasn't hungry and that she did not want to eat dinner, to which Artemis responded, 'It's 7.30 p.m., don't be so silly, of course you must be hungry. I've made your favourite.' That was strike two: emotional boundary violation, via dismissal and ridicule of Electra's feelings. Artemis then went on to say that Electra wasn't taking her life seriously enough and that she was spending too much time with her friends and her boyfriend. That was strike three: social boundary violation, by criticising and trying to control Electra's interactions with her peers. There it was: three strikes and out. Electra started to scream and shout about how she hated her mother's 'shit cooking'. Then she grabbed the tray from Artemis' hands and hurled it out of her bedroom window, where it shattered all over the decking and barbecue area below.

'I was so embarrassed,' said Artemis. 'The neighbours, all watching. What will they think? They will wonder what kind of mother I am. What kind of cook I am, that my food deserves to be thrown out to the birds. I told Electra I'm not cooking for her ever again. And I'm not talking to her. Honestly, she doesn't know what she is talking about! Here, I'll show you.' Artemis opened the tote bag nestled under her arm and took out a squat thermos flask and unscrewed the lid. She leaned across the small space between us and stretched out the arm that was holding the flask. Her eyes were enthusiastically gesturing towards me and it. I didn't need to see it; I could smell it. It was a soup, and I knew exactly what it was: trachanas. It's made with cracked wheat, which has been soaked in yoghurt and dried out. The soup is finished by stirring through cubes of halloumi, which serve as rubbery surprises when you eat it. It has a tangy, sour smell, a bit like bile, and the texture is lumpy. In my family, trachanas has become – not affectionately, but accurately – known as 'sick soup' because it looks like a person on a beige food diet has orally evicted the contents of their gut into your bowl. How Irini Tzortzoglou won MasterChef in 2019 with a main course of lamb chops with trachanas purée is beyond me.

'I can imagine it tastes delicious, Artemis,' I said. My entire face scrunched up because I felt disgusted, but also because I was trying really, really hard to imagine trachanas tasting delicious. I wasn't sure if Artemis wanted me to try some of the soup, but before she got the chance to ask me, I closed the taverna and opened up the therapy room again.

'I'm wondering if we might put the soup aside and continue our conversation,' I said.

'Yes, of course,' Artemis clumsily lidded the soup and put it on the coffee table. She looked a little scrunched herself now. I wondered if she was uncomfortable because we had crossed the boundary from inside the therapy room to the world outside. We had just replayed what was happening at home every night: I had become Electra and had rejected Artemis' food, and therefore Artemis.

But rejection, however hard it is for a parent to bear the brunt of it, is actually about something else during adolescence: the all-important bridge between childhood and adulthood. Adolescents do not need or want to be as physically attached to their caregivers as they were as children. They want to separate from their parents and become their own person. This was exactly what Electra was doing. The attachment paradox of adolescence is that healthy separation from parents doesn't happen through detachment; it happens through secure attachment – and boundaries are the heart of this. However, it's hard to feel secure with someone if you don't know where you stand with them, and I could imagine Electra didn't with her mother: one minute Artemis was hunting Electra down and barging into her room with food; but the next minute, wasn't cooking for her. Artemis couldn't see that she was cutting off her nose to spite her face. If the relationship went on like this, Electra would fly the nest and not come back.

At that moment, as we sat there, I wished that I could cut off my nose; Artemis hadn't completely closed the lid on the thermos flask and the smell of trachanas was wafting in the air. I tried not to inhale, which was difficult, because what I wanted to do most at that moment was sigh. This therapy had barely begun and it already felt like a big fat Greek mess. How was I supposed to do any serious therapeutic work? I felt like I had landed flat on my face, splat, in a bowl of trachanas.

But maybe that's where I needed to start. Julia Child once said, 'What a marvellous resource soup is for the thrifty cook.' (She also said, 'homemade soups fill the kitchen with a welcome air', but she clearly hadn't ever tasted this Greek speciality.)

Julia was right. The soup, and the feelings that were being stirred up with it, were my resource. I decided to be a thrifty therapist.

'I noticed the look on your face when I said about putting the soup aside. I wondered if you may have felt a little upset with me,' I said.

'No, no. I just don't like conflict. Especially with Electra,' Artemis said, as she looked down at the floor. She had used what I had said as a bridge back to her relationship with Electra. So, I followed her lead.

'But it sounds like you and Electra are in conflict much of the time,' I said.

'Yes, and it goes on and on. Round and round. The Electra Problem is what I call it,' said Artemis, doing a loop-the-loop movement with her head.

'That sounds really difficult. It hurts when we're at war with those we love,' I said, feeling my empathy return. Artemis seemed to take my comment; her head was like a nodding dog. I wondered if, now that she felt soothed and seen, she would be open to another way of thinking about conflict. I thought it was worth a shot. 'Sometimes things go round and round and don't get resolved because the feelings underneath are not being understood. Sometimes conflict can be an opportunity to understand what's going on in a relationship, like we're trying to do now with you and Electra. Maybe even with you and me, with what just happened with the soup,' I said, taking the opportunity to bring things back to our therapeutic relationship.

'Conflict never works out,' Artemis said. She wasn't nodding anymore; now she was straight-talking and serious.

'I'm not sure I understand what you mean,' I said.

'I mean conflict. Fighting.' I got the sense that Artemis was talking about something else entirely now. But she quickly retreated and for the rest of our session she shut down any attempt I made to engage her in the emotions behind her statement. By the end, it was clear that Artemis disliked conflict even more than I did trachanas.

***

Artemis apologised at the start of our next session for being late again. The reason was food-related.

'I'm so sorry, Dr Andrea. I was waiting for the baklava to finish in the oven. I wanted to bring you some,' she said, opening up her hessian shopping bag. She took out a large, transparent food container and held it out to me with both hands. This was a first for me, accepting a food gift. A homemade food gift. Inside, I could see honey-coloured cubes of baklava and also its cousin, kataifi, which looked like mini bales of hay. Both types of pastry had been bathed in so much syrup they were glistening like rocks in the sun on Nissi beach in Cyprus. Syrupy desserts are not my favourite thing to eat, but I do love the way the filo pastry in baklava rustles like autumn leaves when you cut through it. And kataifi has inspired many a breakfast. To make my shredded wheat more interesting as a child, I'd either pour on Tate & Lyle's Golden Syrup or my much-loved rosewater cordial, which was so slick and pink it could have been the oil Barbie's Corvette ran on. As a family, we have always had ready-made rather than homemade Greek sweets, because they are not really part of my mother's kitchen repertoire. She was delighted when the famous Greek patisserie, Wilton, opened its doors locally. I didn't share my mother's excitement, but I did think it was funny that they now had branches in the big four baking capitals of the Greek Cypriot world: Larnaca, Limassol, Paphos – and Southgate.

I took the container from Artemis and said thank you as I placed it down on the table between us. Artemis then jolted in her seat, like she'd suddenly remembered something of great importance. She fumbled around in her handbag and took out her phone.

'People always want the recipes for my sweets. They are the original ones from my family in Cyprus. Before we start, shall I just email you the recipes?' said Artemis, her fingers tap dancing on the screen.

This time I didn't get a chance to answer her question. She raised a finger to her lips and mimed a shushing sound. Then she decided when we would resume.

'There! I've emailed them to you.' She looked at me like she had just solved all my problems and that it would be okay to thank her later. 'I hope you enjoy eating and making them, Dr Andrea *mou*.'

There it was. My own three-letter big fat Greek boundary. In my life, *mou* is something I'd only hear from a few people. It's meant to be familial and affectionate, but hearing it from Artemis made me feel like I was a farmyard animal. It wasn't her place to say it. It was like she was invading someone else's territory.

And then it hit me. Splat.

My problem wasn't this small word – it was another word. The C-word in therapy: counter-transference. This is the opposite of transference, when the therapist transfers something or someone onto the patient. It was true that in our work so far, Artemis had been transferring Electra onto me. But right now, Artemis reminded me of someone else and I was also transferring something onto her. There was only one other person in my life who turned up at my door with food and called me 'Andrea *mou*'. That person was my father.

The previous evening, my father had called me to say he 'was just passing by'. (It was clearly a lie. He was at home; I could hear my mother unloading the dishwasher in the background.) My father asked me the same question that he always does: do I 'have food?' Just to put this in context, it's not hard to get hold of food where I live. I have a 24-hour supermarket, a convenience store and an organic food shop all at the end of my road. But my father was being serious. I always turn into an adolescent when he asks me this question. I protested that: one – of course I have food! At the very least, I always have Rice Krispies in the cupboard and actually, snap, crackle and pop are soothing sounds at dinner time after a long day at work; two – he doesn't need to drive all the way here to bring me stuff; and three – I am a fully grown woman who can feed herself. It didn't matter. Three strikes and he was out the door. An hour later he arrived at my house with a bag of Greek groceries. Teetering on top was a steaming hot, sesame-encrusted loaf of *koulouri*. For my father, to 'have food' means eating food that connects me to my Cypriot heritage – and to him. It's what you could call noshtalgia, the food version of nostalgia, which comes from the Greek words *nostos* (to return home) and *algos* (pain).

For my father, his homeland of Cyprus is a painful 'problem' because of the war fifty years ago. He still remembers the day when war broke out, and the way he discovered that his life was going to change forever: his younger sister, hysterically knocking on his door screaming, 'The war is here! The Turks are coming now! You have to go and fight!' My father's name in Greek means freedom, but that was the day he lost his. He's never quite got it back. My father was ordered not only to un-attach from his Turkish friends, but to attack them. Civil war wounds your sense of security in such a cruel way.

I was about to find out that my father and Artemis had the same problem.

There in the session, my own problem with the *mou* comment faded as Artemis began to tell me a story about her baklava and kataifi. When she was growing up her family owned a patisserie, the best and most well-known *zacharo-plasteio* in Kyrenia, a city on the northern coast of Cyprus. It had been in their family for three generations. As soon as Artemis was tall enough to reach the counter, she had started to help out and quickly learned all the pastry tricks of the trade, including how to make gossamer-thin filo pastry. When Turkey invaded Kyrenia in the summer of 1974, Artemis and her family were forced to flee their home. Their patisserie was burned to the ground. Artemis was a teenager when it happened; the same age as Electra was now. Artemis's older brother, like my father, had also been called up for military service, but he never came back. His name remains on the list of missing persons.

The baklava and kataifi in front of me suddenly seemed very bittersweet.

Before the war, everyone knew where they stood. In the family patisserie, some of their customers would ask for *kataifi*, others for *katayif*, but it didn't matter: Greek or Turkish, they were all Cypriots. After the war, that all changed. Cyprus, including its capital city, Nicosia, was sliced in half. There was a line, the Green Line, to tell you who you could love and who you should hate, where you were banished from and where you belonged to. Greeks now belonged to the Republic of Cyprus, Turks to the Turkish Republic of Northern Cyprus. Boundaries became connected with conflict and control. To this day, the 'Cyprus problem' remains unresolved.

But now Artemis had a choice about whether her feelings did.

In therapy, Artemis would see that boundaries could mean something different. If I held the frame, and was there consistently and predictably, Artemis would know what to expect from me and from our work. It was these safe and secure boundaries of our relationship that would help her to explore, express and, eventually, understand her unresolved feelings. Because if you know where you stand with someone, it's safe to go there with them. That is why true boundaries are not barriers; they allow things in, they allow things to open up. In fact, the more secure the boundaries, the more freedom there will be within them – that's the paradox of all relationships, not only the therapeutic one.

Would Artemis bring more food into the therapy room as our work went on? I couldn't predict that. After all, what I had before me was a plastic box, not a crystal ball. But today, Artemis had told me – and shown me – something about what connection was for her, and how her family's food was an important part of that. She had entrusted me with her recipes. It was an act of what attachment researchers call epistemic trust: trust that has personal relevance and helps us to learn about the world. The recipes had helped me to learn something significant about Artemis's world – and my own. Through Artemis, I ended up finding more empathy for my father, which I hoped would help me regress a little less to my adolescent self when I was with him. It had only taken me three decades but I think I'd even found enough empathy to forgive him for singing 'Mary had a little lamb so she killed it and made kebabs' in front of all of my friends at my ninth birthday party.

After I saw Artemis out that day, I walked back into the room and stood for a moment, looking at the plastic box filled with baklava and kataifi. There was a phone call I wanted to make before my next patient. I reached for my bag to find my phone. The number I wanted was at the top of my recent call list; I tapped it and waited.

My father picked up.

This time, it was my turn to say it: 'Dad, I have food.'

* * *

Kataifi Nests

This is my tribute to Artemis' recipe. I thought individual nests, instead of traditional cylinders, were a little more fitting for her story. The milk chocolate chips plus the rose water make these reminiscent of Fry's Turkish Delight, which is my father's favourite chocolate. In my family, kataifi is known as the shredded wheat dessert because the pastry consists of delicate thin strands of filo dough. In case you were wondering, Electra did fly the nest and, with Artemis' blessing, moved out for university. Artemis, of course, gave her lots of meals in plastic containers to take with her.

Makes 12 nests

For the syrup:
170g caster sugar
1 tablespoon rose water
5 cloves

For the filling:
55g chopped almonds
55g chopped walnuts
20g milk chocolate chips
1 tablespoon caster sugar
½ teaspoon vanilla extract
½ teaspoon ground cinnamon
2 teaspoons rose water

For the pastry:
125g kataifi pastry, defrosted if frozen
6 teaspoons olive oil
Sea salt flakes, to garnish

Preheat the oven to 200°C/180°C fan/gas mark 6. Grease the cups of a 12-cup muffin tray with a little oil.

To make the syrup, combine the sugar, rose water and cloves with 225ml water in a saucepan. Bring slowly to a boil, stirring, until the sugar has dissolved. Once it has, stop stirring and boil gently for 5 minutes. Pour into a jug and leave to cool.

Mix the ingredients for the filling together with 1 table-spoon of water and set aside.

Fill a small bowl with water. Wet your hands, then pull a small handful of kataifi strands from the packet and mould them gently into one of the cups of the muffin tray to form a nest. The pastry should approximately half-fill the cups. If your pastry is dry and cracks easily, it might benefit from a quick dip in the water; the pastry strands need to be damp enough to be mouldable in the muffin cup.

Place a generous teaspoon of the filling on top of each kataifi nest base. Then, using the same technique as before, top each one with dampened kataifi strands so that each muffin cup is full.

Sprinkle half a teaspoon of olive oil over each nest. Bake in the oven for 20–25 minutes, or until the nests are golden and crisp.

Remove from the oven and pour over the cooled syrup; each nest will need a generous tablespoon. Allow 30 minutes for the syrup to soak in. Before serving, dot a few sea salt flakes on top of each nest.

7

Black-Eyed Peas:
Where Is the Love?

*What happens when someone breaks
their promise to love you?*

There is a little food song that I sometimes find myself singing. I'm almost ashamed to admit that I know the words by heart. It's not a pop song, but it is about the most popular feeling in the world: love. And although it's not a cheesy song, or a song about cheese, it is about a specific food, which also happens to be very popular. It's actually a jingle, and it featured in a television advertisement a few years before I trained to be a therapist, while I was doing my PhD. So it's been in my memory for many years. The last verse tells the story of a mother who reads the signs that her son is feeling sad and knows exactly the thing to cheer him up: beans. And, as the punchline tells us, Beans Meanz Heinz.

The ad, of course, was for the much-loved cupboard essential that is baked beans.

In my defence, I think at the time I was unconsciously drawn to the baked beans jingle because it was about a little boy's relationship with his mother. So you could say that actually it's about attachment, which is what Heinz has always meant in my life. The women in my family have a lot of love for Heinz. My maternal grandmother, who lived in north London, loved Heinz tinned spaghetti in tomato sauce. My paternal grandmother in southern Cyprus also enjoyed spaghetti with tomato sauce, but Heinz featured in hers slightly differently. Her favourite meal was a pool of cool ketchup on top of a heap of steaming spaghetti. The skin on the tops of her hands was gossamer thin, like ten-denier tights, but she had tough palms that could sure thump a bottle of Heinz tomato ketchup. I spent many of my childhood summer holidays in Cyprus. When we had lunch at my grandmother's house, she would usually sneak a dish of ketchupped spaghetti onto the table – for herself. For everyone else – well, mostly for my father – she made the traditional Cypriot foods that he loved, like *fasolia* (cannellini bean stew, either the plain white version or the red version with tomatoes), *faki* (lentils with rice and onions and lots of olive oil) or revithia (chickpea casserole, a bit like hot, chunky hummus). I would put ketchup on all of them, and they tasted delicious.

Then, of course, there was my mother, who adored the full catalogue of Heinz comestibles, including the condiments, the beans and both Big and little soups. When my father married my mother, he had to accept that baked beans came as part of the deal (I don't think he minded; he thought of it as a 2-for-1). He grew to love the tinned haricot beans stewed in their gluey orange sauce. He learned that Beanz Meanz Heinz. Although in the early days that really didn't help him to learn how to spell in English.

But the beans in my patient Peter's story struck me as mean. Looking at Peter, you might think that he hadn't eaten his beans growing up, or that he'd had much nutrition at all. Peter was waif-like with limp hair, and for a Greek person his skin was surprisingly alabaster, as pale as the Parthenon. Peter was in his thirties, and from what it sounded like, quite developmentally arrested. He still lived with his parents and he spent all day in his room. Peter's life hadn't moved on much as an adult, and when it had moved, it was by command of his mother. Peter's mother had put pressure on him to study law at university, but having failed his first year he couldn't continue with his degree. His mother had been very unhappy about him being a 'dropout'. Since leaving university, Peter had worked part-time as a virtual assistant for a law firm. He wasn't happy in his job, but his mother was happy about still being able to tell people that law was his profession. When Peter wasn't working he was gaming, and he only came downstairs for dinner. Peter had little social life and he didn't leave the house a lot. He had come to see me because he 'felt like a depressed man', and while it was true that Peter had many of the symptoms of depression, to me he felt like a little boy.

In his mother's eyes, Peter had not been a 'good boy' when he was growing up. There was one place in particular where she would say he misbehaved, which was at the dinner table. As a child, Peter would protest against eating his beans, peas and pulses, which in his household did not mean cheery orange tinned baked beans or vibrant green frozen garden peas. Peter said that his mother only cooked 'traditional village food', and the meal she made most often was *louvi* (black-eyed peas), which she would serve with *horta* (wild greens). These beans can be delicious, but only when they are in good hands – and heart. Peter's mother didn't sound like a gentle, a generous or even a good cook. She boiled the beans to death and stewed the greens so much they smelled like sewage. I wondered how Peter's mother had made him eat his beans. Maybe there was something magical that I was missing; after all, he had described her as a witch once, saying she had more of a beard than he did and also a bulbous mole with spiky hairs on her chin. He hated it when she kissed him on the cheek as a child. I pictured her stirring the beans in a cauldron, saying 'Double, double toil and trouble'. As I heard more, it seemed that Peter's mother had used a spell, of sorts: she had used attachment as a force for evil.

'She told me she wouldn't love me anymore and she would leave if I didn't eat my beans,' said Peter, very matter-of-factly. He sounded like he was stating a clause in a contract.

And that's exactly what it was.

Family contracts was something Bowlby wrote about early in his career, before his *Attachment, Separation* and *Loss* books. Although this was some of Bowlby's less well-known work, which he never published, his ideas about promises and implicit contracts in families are compelling. When Peter's mother said to him, 'I won't love you if you don't eat your beans,' she was extracting a promise from Peter. It was an imposed contract. Bowlby was clear about the feeling a child experiences when they violate the family contract by not doing whatever they are told. That feeling is guilt. Peter had tried to explain to his mother that the smell, taste and texture of the beans made him sick, but whenever she stated those terms and conditions, he bowed down. Peter had an obligation to eat his beans. Otherwise, not only would he feel guilt, but he would also fear the punishment his mother threatened: separation. Peter was being force-fed, emotionally and psychologically (even physically on some occasions, when he was very young). There were times when Peter retched right onto his plate. It didn't matter to his mother. She still made him eat those beans. I felt my stomach churn when he said that. It was one of the most disgusting food stories I had ever heard.

Bowlby also said guilt is felt when there is an implicit promise of love plus a pretence that hatred does not exist. Interestingly, in the session where Peter told me about the role of beans in his family contract, he didn't express any hate towards his mother. I found it hard to believe that there was no fire burning inside him, given his experiences. Peter was showing me his moral defence, as therapists would say. Ronald Fairbairn, a colleague of Bowlby's, came up with this concept, saying that it is better 'to be a sinner ruled by God than to live in a world ruled by the Devil'. If your parent is God, rather than the Devil, at least you can hold on to hope and some sense of security, which is what Peter was trying hard to do.

'She was only doing her job,' said Peter, as he cast his eyes down. I could see that Peter thought his job was to make his mother happy. As I heard him speak, I could feel my compassion for the child in him, but it seemed his adult self wasn't seeing this at all.

'Sure, I understand you saying that as an adult, but I'm wondering what the child in you would say,' I said, curious if he could access that part of himself.

Peter didn't respond. About a minute went by, and he still hadn't said anything. Perhaps he was protesting against my question. He lowered his head and turned his whole body away. I decided to teaspoon-feed him some feelings.

'To me, that sounds like the most hurtful thing in the world for a child, to hear that your parent could stop loving you,' I said, dipping my head down so that I could catch his gaze. Peter didn't take in my comment. I noticed that he slightly scrunched his nose up before swiftly moving on to tell me about a time where beans meant something very significant.

Peter hadn't had many friends at school. He was mostly on his own during break times and lunch times, and he was hardly ever invited to anyone's house. Shortly after starting secondary school, Peter had plucked up the courage to invite the two new friends he'd made to his house. He was delighted when they said yes. Then Peter made another bold move: he asked his mother whether, for one night only, she could cook the food he had heard the other children talk about: turkey twizzlers and oven chips and baked beans and spaghetti hoops. Peter told me he wanted to be cool, like the other kids. My ears pricked up at the word 'cool': it had an air of invulnerability about it, as though Peter wanted to be emotionally hardened.

Given what had happened when his friends came round, I could understand why.

When Peter and his friends arrived home that day, they weren't greeted by a waft of warm savouriness. The house had its usual musty smell. While his two friends played games upstairs, Peter asked his mother what they were having for dinner. She said that she had gone to the supermarket earlier, but couldn't bring herself to 'buy that junk'. Instead, she had made their usual food. Peter started to panic, but there was nothing he could do. Half an hour later, he and his friends were sitting at the walnut dining table that was covered with a traditional crochet table cloth, and Peter's mother was dishing out ladlefuls of over-boiled black-eyed peas and greens. When she left the dining room, his friends asked what the food was. Peter told them it was *louvi* – in other words, Greek black-eyed peas. They sniggered and said, 'Loo-vi. It smells like a toilet!' Peter wanted the ground to open up and swallow him there and then, because he knew that wouldn't be the end of it. His friends had fun squashing the beans on their plates, like ants. They only ate bread.

When Peter's mother came back into the dining room, she saw two plates of bean porridge. Peter hadn't touched his food either, in an attempt to be cool. He could see the blood start to boil in his mother's face. She turned to Peter. Then she erupted.

'See, look at you, Peter! This is why you are so scrawny and not growing properly, like a normal boy. You'll never be a man. You never eat your beans or do anything you are told. How dare you disobey your mother? God will punish you and I won't love you anymore. You disgust me.'

As Peter told me this, I felt the sting of every word. Mean was an understatement: Peter's mother had shamed him in front of his friends. They had laughed at him, and left straightaway. As Peter predicted, the toilet jokes continued the next day at school. When the other children got wind of what had happened, they began to yell 'Call the fart brigade!', or sang 'Beans, beans, they're good for your heart. The more you eat, the more you fart' in Peter's presence. Then, when *Toy Story* 2 was released, everyone in class started to call him 'Stinky Pete', like the character in the film. Peter described school as 'hell'. His mother had said this was his punishment for not being a 'good boy'. After that, Peter always ate his beans without putting up a fight.

I could feel my eyes staring wildly at Peter. I tried to explain the look of horrified astonishment on my face.

'This all sounds so hurtful,' I said. It was an astonishingly obvious thing to say, but it was true.

Peter raised and wrinkled his mouth and nose. There it was: that face again. It was another nose scrunch. Peter had made the same facial expression earlier in our session. In fact, he made it every session.

Peter's face was saying: 'Urgh'.

I started to read the signs.

Peter was showing me the classic nose scrunch that psychologists associate with disgust. But disgust doesn't only serve to keep food out – it can keep people out too. Disgust defends against intimacy. That's why some psychologists have said the emotion that is the closest opposite to disgust is love. It looked like Peter was disgusted whenever I expressed any emotion – just like his mother was disgusted when he didn't eat his beans, or when he tried to tell her how he felt. Peter couldn't see the look on his face, as he continued to tell me his feelings about his mother, and himself.

'She was just being a good mother. She is a good mother. Really good. I was just a bad kid,' Peter's eyes were wavering. Then I noticed the colour of his cheeks: he was blushing.

More signs.

There was more than just guilt going on for Peter. A guilty person says, 'I have done something bad'. A shamed person says, 'I am bad'. Shame has been described as disgust turned inwards. It seemed that Peter had internalised all of it: the disgust, the hate, the hurt – even his mother. Peter's face was showing me his shame.

Another of Bowlby's lesser-known works is the biography of Charles Darwin he wrote in his final years. Bowlby believed Darwin's life clearly showed how the loss of an attachment figure affects mental and physical health later on. Darwin's mother died when he was eight years old, and the family did not allow him to talk about her after that. His theory was that Darwin's body 'talked' for him instead with physical symptoms, including panic attacks, anxiety, vertigo, vomiting, headaches and eczema. You could say that Darwin's experience unconsciously influenced his work: his research on how the body shows emotions was an important part of his famous theory of evolution. In his book *The Expression of Emotions in Man and Animals*, Darwin devoted an entire chapter to blushing and the feelings behind it. He wrote that blushing is 'the most human of all expressions', and some have said this is because it's a sign of morality. But I believe it's a sign of vulnerability.

Peter's shame face was his vulnerability.

I could see the redness spreading across Peter's face, slowly extending out to his ears, up his forehead and down his neck. It wasn't what psychologists call a 'classic' blush, which shows suddenly, or a 'flush', like the angry, rapid reddening of Peter's mother's face. This was a 'creeping blush', and it's often seen when someone is being interviewed by a panel or speaking in public – basically those times where you could be judged negatively by others. If you remember from Chapter 4, that's what causes stress: the cortisol response happens on the inside, the blushing happens on the outside, but it's all part of the same system in the body. Darwin said that we blush when we think about what other people think of us. If we think this is negative, the emotion we tend to feel is shame.

I wondered what Peter thought I was thinking of him now. Perhaps he was thinking that if he wasn't a good boy, who thought of his mother as good, then he would be in trouble with me. But I felt that now was not the time to force-feed him too many of my interpretations. Today had shown me that we needed to take baby steps. Peter and I had only been working together for two months, so it was still early days. In this session, however, we had started to see the shameful feelings behind those beans, which had become so engrained in him. He had shown me something important about how he had been loved, and therefore what he needed: not just compassion, but permission. Peter needed permission to truly reveal himself, and to be the boy who did not eat his beans, without the fear of shaming judgement or separation. In therapy, Peter could have an experience of me as a 'mother' who read the signs and saw him and accepted him for who he was. My hope began here. Peter had the possibility of a different relationship with me, one in which he didn't have to say to himself, 'I must be a good patient otherwise Andrea won't be my therapist'. It was going to take time and understanding to undo the attachment spell and Peter's 'contractual' obligations, but it's always best to go slow in therapy and to have patience as the process unfolds. I think it was another Heinz advertisement that said: 'The best things come to those who wait.'

* * *

Greek Baked Beans

Not Heinz and not tinned, but seriously good. This is my family's version of baked beans, in other words, *fasolia*. I like to eat these beans non-Greek style, i.e., on toast or on top of a jacket potato, or even as part of a full English breakfast.

Serves 4

3 tablespoons olive oil
1 medium onion, peeled and finely chopped
4 medium celery sticks, cut into 1cm slices
4 medium carrots, peeled, quartered lengthways and
    cut into 1cm slices
2 medium courgettes, quartered lengthways and cut
    into 1cm slices
1 tablespoon tomato purée
1 teaspoon tomato ketchup
25g flat-leaf parsley, finely chopped
500g frozen cannellini beans or 2 x 400g cans cannellini
    beans, drained

1 x 400g tin plum tomatoes, crushed (use your hands or
  a fork)
750ml vegetable stock
1½ teaspoons salt
½ teaspoon ground pepper

Heat the olive oil in a large saucepan. Add the onion, celery, carrots and courgettes. Cook gently for around 5 minutes over a medium heat.

Stir in the tomato purée, tomato ketchup, parsley and cannellini beans and cook for a further 2 minutes.

Add the crushed tomatoes, vegetable stock, salt and pepper. Swill out the tomato tin with a little warm water to get all the juice, and add that too.

Bring to the boil, then reduce to a simmer and cover the pan. Let the beans bubble away for around 30–40 minutes until they are soft enough to crush with your fingers and their sauce has thickened. Serve as you would baked beans.

8

It's Not Just Lunch

*How can you stop the green-eyed monster
from hurting your relationship?*

My patient Ella usually had a tiny little voice. Sometimes I could only just hear it. But today her voice had become big, and it was becoming bigger as our session went on. It then grew so big that it was almost a growl. As I listened to her and her great, rough, gruff voice, I almost expected her next words to be, 'Someone's been eating my porridge!' But despite the fact that she sounded like Father Bear, and also that she looked like Goldilocks, porridge was not the issue in Ella's food story. It wasn't breakfast, either.

It was a lunch issue.

'I wouldn't have minded if it was just a drink,' said Ella, practically shouting. She had a point. The anthropologist Mary Douglas has a lot to say about drinks compared to meals. In her opinion, the rules are clear: drinks are for strangers, contractors and acquaintances; meals are for family, romantic partners and close friends. Her idea is actually rooted in attachment theory because it's about the line between intimacy and distance, between seeking more or less closeness. If we only know someone over drinks, we know them less (and we may not even like them at all). But once food is on the table, so is love. I like Douglas because she's like a detective; in her paper *Deciphering a Meal* she says that food is a code. Meals have meaning. Cocktails, coffee and tea are simple categories of drinks, but they don't have the power to structure our day like the events of breakfast, lunch and dinner. For Ella, the lunch that had happened felt like a big event. And in our session she was trying to decode the message behind it.

'I can't believe they went there. There are a million other places they could have gone to. Why does she want to eat lunch with Tristan anyway? He's mine. Not hers. And if they had to eat lunch together, why did they go there? There? It's our place. Ours. Not theirs. Mine and his. Ours. Together. Not hers.' Each pronoun packed a punch as it came out of Ella's mouth. However, beneath her big voice, I could hear the tiny voice of vulnerability. Now she felt like Baby Bear.

Ella had just found out that her boyfriend, Tristan, had been to 'their' place for lunch last week with someone else: his colleague Cassie. Tristan hadn't mentioned this to Ella because he thought it wasn't a big deal. In his mind, the restaurant was near his office and therefore convenient for lunch. Ella had burst into tears when Tristan told her the other day. Her upset hadn't dissipated, and she had become increasingly possessive ever since: three times already this week, Ella had made Tristan cancel plans with his friends and stay in with her.

In Ella's mind, there was a lot more to this than just lunch. Their place was a Greek restaurant that I happened to know well. I have to say, at this restaurant the lunch is very good. I remember I had the midweek mini meze, but there was nothing mini about it. Whether I've had lunch or dinner at this place, I have been well fed. The décor is interesting too. It's not exactly old-world taverna charm; there are high-back faux-leather dining chairs and crisply ironed white table cloths, which give a certain formality. After all, eating Greek is serious business. But sharing food, like meze or family style, also has serious psychological and emotional effects, because you could end up sharing minds. Research tells us that sharing food, whether it's tortilla chips and salsa or crackers or French fries or even soup, tends to promote empathy, trust and closeness between people. Leaving your romantic partner out of a meal will elicit much more jealousy than having a coffee without them. In light of that, I could see why Ella's feelings felt too hot, too big and too hard.

Ella didn't know about that research, but psychologists have discovered something else about mealtimes that she might have found comforting. One study found that evening meals are better for building relationships than lunch, the interpretation being that nightfall makes social activities more enchanting and engaging. The first time Ella and Tristan went to their place was for dinner about a year and a half ago. After dating for a few weeks, this was to be the night when they decided to be 'exclusive'. For Ella, this had added magic because it was a first; she'd never had a long-term relationship before or someone she could call her boyfriend. Ella was in her mid-twenties and she lived on her own in a small flat with her cat, Mog ('me and Mog' was something she said often). She had a job as a computer programmer but since she hated the hot-desk system in the office, she worked from home most of the time. During the day, Ella would often take her laptop to the local café and work from there, which is how she met Tristan; his office was on the same street as the café. So their relationship had started with coffee. Then cocktails. It hadn't taken long for them to progress to breakfast, lunch and dinner.

I remember Ella telling me about the first time they had gone to their Greek restaurant. It was one of the hottest days of the year, and Ella had decided to sunbathe in her garden; she wanted her skin to be tanned for her date with Tristan that evening. As she lay on her front reading her book, Ella had fallen asleep in the sunshine. She had over-done the sun, and didn't quite end up with the healthy golden glow she was looking for. From Ella's description, I imagined her back looked like beef carpaccio.

Ella said she was in a great deal of pain by the time she met Tristan for their date, but she 'did a good job of hiding it'. At the restaurant, they ordered the meze, the non-lunch maxi version, which I have also had before. There are always too many starters for the size of the table, so some have to be precariously balanced on top of each other: little dishes of *taramasalata, hummus, tahini, tzatziki, fava, melinzanosalata* and *tyrokafteri*. Those are just the dips. There are also *gigandes, fasolaki*, tabbouleh, olive-oiled boiled potatoes, lemon and parsley-flecked shredded crabstick, a little seafood salad of octopus, prawns and mussels, lightly pickled baby mushrooms and dark violet chunks of vinegary beetroot. And pitta too.

Ella and Tristan's date had started well, not only in terms of food. They were getting on like a house on fire. Everything was wonderful, except for the fact that Ella's sunburn was becoming more and more painful as the night went on. She wasn't hiding her pain as well as she thought. Tristan noticed that Ella kept wincing. He asked her what was wrong, but she just kept saying she was 'fine' (I could imagine Ella saying this; she frequently used that word in our sessions). As their meze meal went on, Tristan was like a dog with a bone, and persisted in asking Ella what was the matter. Ella had managed to keep her fineness going until the fish course. She finally told Tristan that her skin was as charred and blistered and red as the barbecued red mullet in front of them. The shame of telling him how 'stupid' she had been felt hot like her sunburn. Ella wasn't prepared for Tristan's reaction: he immediately called the waiter over and asked for a little takeaway foil container. Then he started spooning the leftover tzatziki into it. Ella was confused. Tristan said that yoghurt, especially Greek yoghurt, was an excellent remedy for burns. He told Ella not to worry: he was going to take care of her sunburn, and of her. He was gallant and gentle as he helped her home. Later that night, Tristan asked Ella to officially be his girlfriend. Not only had the tzatziki helped to heal her skin, but perhaps you could say it also played a part in Ella and Tristan's exclusivity as a couple, and how this Greek restaurant became their place.

I wish this was the only story about tzatziki I know. Unfortunately, it isn't. The other one is from when I was a child on holiday in Cyprus. We were having lunch one day at my grandmother's house and the whole family was there – so around twenty people. I must have been about eleven years old. My cousin Pandora was around fourteen years old. At the table, Pandora would not stop fidgeting in her chair. I mean, it was incessant: she could not sit still. And her facial movements too: she looked like a baby breaking wind and bouncing in a walker at the same time. My grandmother asked Pandora's mother, my aunt Antigone, what the problem was. My aunt didn't hold back in telling her that poor Pandora really did have something in her box: she had a yeast infection *kato* ('underneath'). My grandmother mobilised into earth-mother mode. She shouted down to Pandora, who was sitting all the way at the other end of the table, 'Pandora *mou*, I used all the yoghurt in the tzatziki, but take the leftovers and use it to soothe your infection down below. The cucumber and the garlic will help too.' Everyone went silent and put down their knives and forks – and it takes a lot for hungry Greek folk to do that. Pandora went whiter than the yoghurt. In some sort of physiologically empathic response to her, my cheeks became as crimson as the tomatoes my grandmother grew in her garden. Anyway, Pandora did as she was told, and the tzatziki must have worked wonders because she came to the beach with us the next day for the first time that holiday. However, as you might imagine, I have never looked at tzatziki in the same way ever since.

As I sat with Ella in our session, I could see there was a feeling burning inside her, and it was something that no amount of tzatziki could calm. It was jealousy. And it was a jealousy of Shakespearean proportions, it would seem. The green-eyed monster in Ella had fed her the idea that because Tristan had taken Cassie to their place, she was now his exclusive work colleague, lunch buddy – or more. Ella was so enraged that she had gone to the restaurant the other day to ask Stavros, the manager, about Tristan and Cassie's lunch.

'I didn't care if Stavros thought I was a nut job, I needed to know what happened. It was like I was possessed,' Ella said, her voice rising on the word 'possessed'.

Ella must have used her big growly voice, because Stavros told her every detail about what Tristan and Cassie had eaten (the mini meze, but without any dishes containing dairy because Cassie said she was lactose intolerant); what time they'd arrived (12.40 p.m.); what time they'd left (1.25 p.m.); and if they had taken any leftovers with them (they hadn't). Ella had even asked if Cassie looked sunburned (Stavros said no, and reminded her that it was December). Even though the evidence added up to just lunch, Ella wasn't soothed. She still doubted Tristan and the meaning of the meze lunch. I wondered if Ella was doing as the paediatrician and psychoanalyst Donald Winnicott said: using her doubt about food to hide her doubt about love. Maybe I was being the detective now. I suspected that Tristan was a placeholder for some unconscious need from Ella's childhood that hadn't been fed.

Bowlby opened the second volume of his trilogy, *Separation*, by discussing jealousy in children. He described how infants and young children in residential nurseries during World War Two would become acutely jealous whenever 'their' nurse gave attention to another child. They were clingy, strongly possessive, unwilling to be left for a minute and continually demanding. Some would lie on the floor, sobbing. It appeared that Ella's behaviour wasn't any different, and neither was the feeling driving it. Just like those children, Ella felt that her attachment relationship was being threatened by a third party.

Jealousy tends to involve three people: an individual, an attachment figure and a rival. These are the ingredients of what classical psychoanalysis calls the oedipal situation, which happens in childhood around the ages of three to five. Bowlby didn't talk much about this in attachment theory because at the time he was trying to pull away from people like Freud, who were talking about it a lot, in quite sexual terms (attachment theory is pretty unsexy, as theories go).

In therapy, we don't tend to use the word 'oedipal' either. But much of this stuff can be reinterpreted in attachment terms because it's about separation and loss. We all start life as a pair with our attachment figure: it's a time of 'me and you'. Just us. But as a child, we learn that our loved one is not only ours, and we are not only theirs. We must eventually separate from our special twosome. The shape that is important in this lifelong lesson is the triangle. There will always be a pair, what psychologists call a 'dyad', and an excluded party. We have to negotiate triangles throughout life, and it's not just the typical case of Father Bear, Mother Bear and Baby Bear. There are different types of triangles.

This was something I realised as a child.

One summer, a few years before the tzatziki incident with my cousin Pandora, Madonna's song 'Papa Don't Preach' was number one. My mother recorded it for me on video and I watched it over and over again. I took the tape on holiday to Cyprus with me, where Pandora and I watched it together, over and over again. Pandora wanted to perfect the dance moves, but I had no interest in that. Much to Pandora's annoyance, I kept rewinding and watching the scene in the video when Madonna serves her father dinner, trying to figure out what they were eating. I basically did this every day for the whole holiday. I was completely and utterly obsessed with the food and the father-daughter dynamics, to the point that I misunderstood the song. I thought when Madonna sang the lyrics, 'I'm keeping my baby,' she meant her boyfriend, and that she was trying to tell her father, over dinner, that she was walking out the door because of that. So I asked myself: What would you cook for someone if you're going to break the bad news that you're leaving them? Mashed potatoes, of course. If anything was going to soften the blow that Madonna was choosing to keep her boyfriend and not her preachy father, it was that. For years and years, I was convinced they were eating mashed potatoes (I'm not so sure now, having seen the video again recently). It turns out that the song was more literal than I thought, and what Madonna was keeping actually *was* a baby. But whether Madonna was leaving her father behind for her boyfriend or her baby or both, my childhood concern was the same: Madonna's poor papa! Who was going to make him mashed potatoes now?

That's the thing with triangles: sooner or later someone gets left out. But that's life.

And that was the first time I became aware of oedipal edible issues.

Some say that our first taste of exclusion in childhood is sibling rivalry, which arises from competition for parentally provided 'food'. Sometimes first children can be jealous of the attention showered on new-born 'rival' siblings. I have often wondered about this in relation to my older brother. I don't think he was too happy when I came into the world during the oedipal stage of his life, when he was in his first triangle with our mother and father. I was the rival who threw him off his first-born throne (unconsciously, that is, not literally). Although my brother was a bit of a Greek prince. He wasn't born like that; he was made like that. The reason for this was onions. In my family, often there were usually large chunks of raw onion strewn over the table to accompany your meal, for health benefits. I think it stemmed from the ancient belief that they were fed to the troops of Alexander the Great, as it was thought they provided strength to soldiers. When we were growing up, my big brother ate a lot of onions in the hope that they would make him big and strong and Great. If there happened to be no onions on the table, then my brother would casually say, 'An onion would go well with this, wouldn't it?' Oh no it wouldn't, because that potent sulphury flavour will completely and utterly kill your lunch. But that was really just code for 'get me and peel me and chop me an onion'. See? A real prince.

Ella was the older sibling in her family. As a child, she was always forced to share everything with her younger brother, Max, including her food; Max was a 'growing lad', as her father would say, and he needed feeding more than Ella. I wondered if this was a case of not enough food to go round, or not enough love. Ella's father was a traditional Father Bear. He was the breadwinner, and her mother stayed at home. It seemed that Ella's mother had looked after the house more than she had Ella and Max. Ella said her mother was 'completely OCD' and that 'she spent all day cleaning with Mr Muscle and Mr Sheen'. It sounded like Ella's mother was in a triangle of her own. This left Ella and Max competing for their father's love and attention. Except it felt to me that Ella had lost from the start, even before Max came along. On the day Ella was born, her father had dropped her mother off to hospital in labour, on his way to work. When Ella told me this, I felt my own feelings rise at the words 'dropped off'. I visualised the scene as a 'Bye! Have a nice time, sweetheart!' drive-by, as if her mother was a child going to holiday camp. But for Max, Ella's father had been present every step of the way. Ella suspected it was because Max was a boy. For both pregnancies, her father had wanted to know the sex of the baby. Max was named after Ella's paternal grandfather, but Ella, on the other hand, had been named after a woman at the supermarket checkout. When Ella's father came to the hospital the day after Ella was born, he had stopped on the way to buy a box of chocolates for Ella's mother. The lady at the checkout's nametag had 'Ella' written on it.

Ella's belief that Max was favoured had unconsciously created lifelong feelings of inadequacy, invisibility and unlovability in her. She had no confidence in her value. The patriarchal dynamics also added something very sour to the mix. Despite what Ella had said to me about her behaviour in relation to Tristan's lunch with Cassie – that she was 'possessed'– the irony was that she wasn't: that was the problem. Ella had never had the experience of 'just us', so when Max arrived it was like rubbing salt into an already salted wound. Now that Ella had found this feeling with Tristan and their place, she wasn't going to lose it – to Cassie or to anyone else.

It's important to say that jealousy is different from envy: jealousy is the wish to not share whereas envy is the desire to destroy. Ella didn't have a grand plan to ruin Cassie by secretly spiking her coffee with cow's milk, but if Ella shared Tristan with her, that could threaten their relationship. Sharing might mean separation. What Ella was experiencing was extreme separation anxiety, and her clinging and covert lunch surveillance were ways of coping. Researchers would say these were hyperactivating attachment strategies – in other words, highly energised, intensified responses to what feels like a life-or-death situation. I noticed today that even Ella's hair seemed hyper: her sleek, separate ringlets of hair had formed into a thicket of frizz.

When we need to survive, our attachment system activates. Ella's jealous behaviour was really attachment behaviour. Ella was trying to protect a relationship that, for her, felt vital to her survival. It was all in the name of love. Winnicott also said that if children have no capacity to love, then they don't show jealousy. So jealousy is love gone wrong, and one of those times where attachment behaviour makes sense, but has no sense. As Maya Angelou once told us: 'Jealousy in romance is like salt in food. A little can enhance the savour, but too much can spoil the pleasure and, under certain circumstances, can be life-threatening.'

Ella later told me about a certain threat she had made.

'I told Tristan he's not allowed to go to that restaurant, not with her. Not with anybody ever again. Just us. It's our meze. He can only go with me,' said Ella. I gave her the space to hear herself. Her big voice had now been replaced with a big demand, one that could end up over-salting and spoiling her relationship with Tristan. It was another hyperactivating strategy – the strategy of a child who couldn't bear to be excluded or separated.

I think we had started to crack the code of lunch at their place. Ella did not want to share the meze or the restaurant or Tristan – or, originally, her father. Because what the green-eyed monster of jealousy demands is exclusivity. Ella was longing for the exclusive love that she had never had from a man.

Of course, there was one other person Ella shared: me. I wondered what fantasies she had about her fellow 'sibling' patients. Later on in our session, I found myself sharing this very thought with Ella.

'I wonder how it feels to you that I have other patients,' I said.

'Well, once when I was walking down the road after our session, I saw a girl with dead straight black hair and she looked sad. I imagined she might be coming to see you. I know you have other patients,' Ella said with a small smile, as if she was trying to let me know that it was okay.

'I know you know that I do. But I wonder how it feels,' I said.

'I feel fine,' said Ella. I wasn't convinced. If Ella wasn't fine about someone else eating her meze, then she was unlikely to be fine about the fact that someone else would soon be sitting in her chair. 'Fine' was a good place to put those feelings

Ella wasn't using her voice to name: anger, disappointment, sadness. Still, we would have to continue that story another time: this was our last session before the Christmas break, so Ella and I would be separating for a little while.

At the end of our session, Ella took out a tin of chocolates and popped them casually on the coffee table. There was a bow stuck on top and also a gift tag, which read, 'Merry Christmas Andrea! Love, Ella!' The exclamation marks didn't feel like her big bear voice; it felt like a sweet message from someone who wanted to be seen. Over the festive season, I would see and think of Ella each time I reached for a chocolate. Maybe you could say that, through food, Ella had made her way into *my* place. Ella didn't know it, but there was an element of exclusivity here: Ella was the only patient who ever gave me a Christmas gift. She had done the same last year too, although the chocolates were different. Of all the chocolates Ella could have chosen, this year she gave me Quality Street. Not Roses, or Heroes, or Celebrations, but Quality Street: the only box of chocolates in the world that includes the Green Triangle.

And that's exactly what I ate after Ella left.

* * *

Watermelon Tzatziki

Although I have never felt the same way about tzatziki after what happened with my cousin, this version I quite like, as a refreshing riff on the original meze dish. I just want to say, as a caveat: this is for eating. Whether it has any other soothing, medicinal or health benefits for other parts of the body, I cannot say.

Serves 8–10

400g watermelon flesh (skin removed)
2 tablespoons cider vinegar
½ clove garlic
500g Greek yoghurt
3 tablespoons extra virgin olive oil
1 teaspoon dried mint
½ teaspoon salt (plus an extra pinch)
Freshly milled pepper (pink if you have it, for its colour and fruitier flavour)

Grate the watermelon on the coarsest side of the box grater (don't grate it down to a pulp; you want juicy threads of pink dispersed throughout the dip). Place the watermelon flesh in a bowl with one tablespoon of the cider vinegar and a pinch of salt. Stir and set aside for a few minutes.

Crush the garlic and stir it into the yoghurt. Stir in the rest of the vinegar, olive oil, dried mint, salt and a couple of grinds of pepper.

Put the grated watermelon in a muslin cloth or a couple of sheets of strong kitchen roll and squeeze out any excess liquid. Add the flesh to the yoghurt mixture and stir well. Serve with pitta.

9

Heartburn

*Would you use food as a weapon against
your loved one?*

My patient Rachele was telling me what she had cooked
for her husband the other night: ragù with pasta. Her recipe was different from what is hailed as the original ragù
alla Bolognese, that of Italian writer and businessman
Pellegrino Artusi, given in his 1891 magnum opus *Science
in the Kitchen and the Art of Eating Well*. Rachele's was a
family recipe, passed down from her mother in Italy, and
she had cooked it hundreds of times during her thirty-year
marriage. This was certainly no spag bol. Nor did it resem-
ble my own mother–daughter memories of cooking pasta
with tomato sauce, where my favourite culinary task as
a child was to over-enthusiastically squeeze the tube of
tomato purée into the pan. There were no squeezy tubes in
Rachele's kitchen; she used San Marzano tomatoes to make
her own purée. She had several jars stored in the pantry.

The first step of Rachele's ragù involved browning
veal bones and using them to make a rich, dark, gelatinous stock. She always minced the organic veal herself

because, in her words, she 'did a much better job of it' than the butcher, who was 'useless'. She followed her mother's recipe to the letter, which included adding only one and a half bay leaves and exactly eight gratings of whole nutmeg. The sauce simmered away patiently and slowly on the stove all afternoon. In the meantime, Rachele took care of the pasta, which she always made fresh. This time it was tagliatelle. I imagined Rachele rolling the dough through the machine and using her perfectly manicured fingers, tipped with blood-red nails, to vigorously tousle the blond ribbons that came out the other side. Dinner was all set. All Rachele needed now was for her husband to return home from work.

Rachele's husband was also Italian – let's call him Marco, in line with the title of this chapter and the character of Mark in Nora Ephron's novel *Heartburn*. (FYI, the film version has a different pasta trajectory to my story here: carbonara, rather than ragù.)

As Rachele heard Marco's car pull into the driveway, she finished off the ragù with a final thought and an ingredient that was *not* part of her family recipe, which she revealed to me with gusto. Her exact words were: 'I thought, fuck him, and threw a load of chilli into his dinner!' The finishing touches were Scotch bonnets, bird's eye chillies, cayenne pepper and Tabasco. She had more or less dumped the entire chilli contents of her cupboard and fridge into the sauce. Why? Because Marco had dumped her, emotionally: he was having an affair.

Rachele and I had been working together for about a month before this incident – the culinary one, not the infidelity. The affair had been going on for some time. I'd had an inkling that something was being concealed, not only by Marco; Rachele was always perfectly covered up with a lot of make-up. She was the most glamorous patient I'd ever had. She was in her fifties, petite and very beautiful, with 1980s chic. Her signature Chanel No. 5 scent had a strong top note of cigarette smoke. Even her rage was stylish, as though it had strutted off the catwalk straight into the consulting room. Her anger had attitude, especially during the session when she told me about the chilli-spiked sauce. Marco's dinner was not the only target of Rachele's rage.

'I want to chop his dick off.' She looked straight at me with steely anger.

I was unsure how to reply. Clearly the therapist stock phrase, 'I can see you're angry,' wasn't quite going to cut it.

I was silent.

Rachele was far from silent. She was on a rampage. The temperature of the session grew hotter and hotter. I was worried she would burst into flames as she went on to talk about what she had done before cooking dinner. She had cut the crotch out of every single pair of Marco's trousers. I found myself thinking about the American therapist Lori Gottlieb, who initially trained in medicine. In her book *Maybe You Should Talk to Someone?*, she describes dissecting a cadaver's penis at med school by making 'a vertical incision along the entire base of the penis, so that it split open into two neat halves, like a hotdog.' I had a fleeting thought that if Marco had walked in on Rachele while she was holding the scissors, his penis would have suffered a similar fate and ended up in a bun. Rachele would probably have put chilli sauce on that, too.

Marco's trousers were where the affair had been confirmed. Before her spontaneous scissor frenzy, Rachele had been going about the laundry as usual when she felt something unusual in Marco's pocket. Inside, she had found four little blue pills. Rachele and Marco hadn't had sex since their youngest child was born. That child was now eighteen and had left for university around the time Rachele came to therapy. I'd never had the impression of Marco as a virile, Adonis-type from Rachele's descriptions of him. She said Marco had a delicate, 'kiddy' palate; he hated spicy foods.

As in the title of Artusi's book, and in Rachele's behaviour that day, there was indeed science in the kitchen (but nobody was eating well). I have heard this story before — not in the therapy room, but in the lab during my days as a researcher. Rachele had, unbeknownst to her, enacted the hot sauce paradigm. Psychologists use this to assess aggression, by measuring the amount of hot sauce purposely doled out to a target known to dislike fiery foods. The hot sauce paradigm has revealed interesting things about those who have a specific attachment characteristic: fear of rejection. Bowlby said that we can survive the experience that our hate may drive a person away, but to have one's love rejected is intolerable. Rejection is one of the most, if not the most, painful experiences for a human being. People who are anxious about, or feel any risk of, rejection are more likely to have fight-or-flight reactions. Examples of fight behaviours include impulsive and retaliatory anger using any weapon (or, in Rachele's case, condiment) you can get your hands on. As they say, hell hath no fury like a scorned woman holding a bottle of hot sauce.

Instead of feeling her pain, Rachele was projecting it outwards, which is something often seen in therapy, and in life. Projection is our way of playing hot potato with our feelings. If you don't like your emotions or parts of your personality, you unconsciously give them to other people to hold. For example, a person who feels rejected and unwanted becomes very rejecting of others around them. That way, someone else feels the feeling instead. Projection is a defence: if Rachele projected all these feelings outwards onto Marco, then she could avoid looking inwards, at who she was and what she had brought to the table throughout their relationship.

Rachele wanted Marco to feel the burn of rejection, which he did literally when he ate the ragù – he projected it out instantly and vomited all over the kitchen. But it was more than this one incident. Rachele had been giving Marco a taste of her feelings throughout their marriage. He frequently felt the burn of Rachele's words: most days she named, blamed or shamed him in some way for not being good enough. The problem with naming and shaming is that it doesn't stop people doing what they are doing; it just stops them from admitting it. Much like Mark in *Heartburn* (who also cheated on Rachel – their marital trajectory was the same), Marco had lied and bullshitted. Psychologists have actually found differences between the two: liars make false claims about what is true, whereas bullshitters sometimes don't even know what the truth is. The two are not mutually exclusive and individuals who have complicated psychological lives will often be both.

The other problem with projection is that when someone else feels the feeling you give them, they might identify with it – and act on it. I like to think of this as supersized projection. It's what we call 'projective identification'. Now Marco had become the rejector by having an affair with another woman. In the process, he had given the original hot potato right back to Rachele.

I gazed gently at Rachele as she vented about Marco and his 'piece of shit on the side'. She stopped for breath and returned my gaze with a glare. She lowered and drew together her pencil-thin eyebrows. I sensed another attack was imminent. Before Rachele resumed her rant, I invited her to consider something.

'Maybe on some level, deep down, you knew what Marco was up to. You saw it, but it was just too painful to really look at,' I said.

I gave Rachele time to take in what I had said, and after a few moments it was as though some very distant bells started to ring much more loudly. She began to list the red flags she had seen over the last few years: the unidentified numbers on the phone bills, the times when Marco would disappear at weekends and his phone would be off for hours, the receipts for perfume from duty free and for hotels and restaurants, the times when he would have to fly to the Milan office at short notice (there was no Milan office, as it turned out). Rachele hadn't batted an eyelid. She had never questioned anything. I remembered the first line of Artusi's book: 'See how often human judgement errs.' But for Rachele, there was a clear reason why this had been the case: she was afraid of being rejected – that was her real anxiety deep down. If a person fears rejection they will tend to stay in neglectful or even emotionally abusive relationships, simply because it feels less hurtful than being rejected. But this denies what's really going on in the relationship. Denial, just like anger, is a way of distancing. But anger can also be a way of trying to bring someone closer.

I shared my thinking with Rachele.

'Sometimes our anger can be a protest, a way of saying "stay with me but don't do that again",' I said.

Rachele, however, insisted this wasn't the case. Her response was short and spicy. 'No, I wanted to burn him. Just like he did to me.'

I told Rachele I understood that. At the end of the day, hurt people hurt people. In the silence that followed, I found myself trying to understand Rachele's anger. Bowlby said the 'anger of hope' can actually protect and promote a relationship: the anger serves as a way of seeking closeness, so it stops separation. Perhaps this was one side of Rachele's hot sauce story. But it seemed that another part of her was showing what Bowlby called 'the anger of despair'. Over time, Rachele had become so persistently and intensely angry with Marco that her anger had crossed the line to become aggressive and alienating, as well as revengeful. Their bond had weakened. I wondered if it had ever been there in the first place; if she had ever really let Marco in. After all, Rachele's hot-sauced rage told me how sensitive she was to rejection, and she had seemingly struggled with this since her early years.

The first time we met, Rachele talked about 'the shell'. She said, 'There's this shell around me that's been built up. It's been there for as long as I can remember. Nobody gets into the shell. It's the way I work.' As I tried to picture her shell, two images came to my mind: a tortoise with her home and her identity on her back, providing her protection, but weighing her down at the same time. Or the shell of a Kinder Egg: childlike and crackable, where the surprise inside the angry shell was her vulnerability. Anger is the ultimate 'show don't tell' feeling. Because we don't really want to tell ourselves or others that inside we feel hurt and vulnerable and insecure.

In our current session, after about a minute, Rachele broke the silence.

'I don't care anymore. I'm not afraid to lose him,' Rachele said. She pressed her lips tightly together.

I wondered to myself what Rachele was afraid to lose, if it wasn't her relationship with Marco. Both anger and anxiety are responses to the risk of loss, and the hurt this causes. Anxiety is the expectation of being hurt, anger is the expression of being hurt. Both emotions have the same goal, which is essentially to keep you safe. But if Rachele and Marco separated, she wouldn't be safe; she would lose who she was. Who was she, if she wasn't the good wife who made the ragù exactly as her mother taught her to? Rachele had dedicated her life to this role. She filled our sessions with stories of elaborate dinners she cooked for Marco, as if she was trying to show me what a good wife she was, no doubt because inside she didn't feel good enough. I was curious to know whether this was the story of Rachele's life – I wondered if behind the good wife was a good daughter who was trying to please her parent. Rachele then told me that when she got married, her mother had told her to be a 'good housewife'. Specifically, Rachele should 'stand in the kitchen and cook it, get on her knees and clean it, lie down and take it'. It might have been the era of Free Love, but all Rachele had learned from her attachment figure was that love had a high price, and was paid for with a list of 'shoulds': she should be good, she should cook, she should forgo her own feelings to serve others, she should not be herself. As I listened to Rachele, I thought to myself, *she should be angry*. How could she not be? There was a lot to be angry about because there was a lot to lose – and the biggest loss at stake seemed to be the identity she had created for herself over the last thirty years.

'Maybe you're not afraid of losing Marco. Perhaps it's about losing something else,' I said.

Rachele's eyes wavered. Then they blinked repeatedly, as if she was trying to shoo away her vulnerability – and me. I was worried I had cracked the shell. Maybe she was scared that I might take her anger away. It looked like she was holding on to it. Her hands were in her lap and she held one fist with the other, in what looked like a desperate, heavy-handed hug.

No: Rachele had a right to her anger and it was not my place to try to manoeuvre it or change it. That would just add to her sense of loss. What I could do was offer a space to think about it. But that would only come after she had felt what she needed to feel. Our brain feels before it thinks. At some point, though, we would have to move beyond her letting off steam. We had to, otherwise she would stay stuck. I hoped in time that we could work towards a place where Rachele could think about her anger, how it was driven by her constant, anxious anticipation of being let down and the vulnerability that was at the heart of it. Being aware of her anger in this way, instead of actually 'being' her anger and acting it out, would allow Rachele to feel that she had choices: things she could do, instead of should do. This would then give her the freedom to do things differently going forward – if she wanted to, of course.

I knew that as the therapy went on, Rachele's anger would likely come out towards me in some form, be it criticism, irritation, frustration or fury. However, I also hoped that if I showed her this was a relationship where she didn't have to fear rejection, that when she did express her anger she could serve it to me without hot sauce. If Rachele felt safe enough, then she might even let me into the shell – one day.

Rachele then responded to me with a statement that was in keeping with our conversation that day: 'I'm not afraid of losing anything. But he should be afraid of losing his dick.'

Clearly, we were some way off being able to talk about Rachele's vulnerability. I took a deep breath. My job, today, was to let Rachele be emotional and to contain all of the feelings spuming out of her, while keeping my compassion on a steady simmer. For the rest of our session, Rachele remained on a rollicking boil and, unlike Mark in *Heartburn*, called her spouse more than 'a shrew and a bitch and a nag and a kvetch and a grouse'. A lot more.

***

Tyrokafteri Tagliatelle

I can't think of a more appropriate recipe to accompany Rachele's story. *Tyrokafteri* combines two Greek words: *tyro* means 'cheese' and *kaftero* means 'burning hot'. This is fiery, spicy hot. It is supposed to (somewhat) blow your head off. Traditionally, *tyrokafteri* is served as a dip. But it is so much better as a sauce for pasta, which here feels like an homage to the carbonara in the film *Heartburn*, and also to Rachele – the 'nduja is the extra Italian spicy touch in my version. Feel free to substitute the tagliatelle with spaghetti. You might feel some burn when you eat this, but it won't be of the heart kind.

Serves 4

1 red bell pepper
400g tagliatelle
200g feta
40g 'nduja
2 tablespoons olive oil
2 tablespoons full-fat Greek yoghurt (the higher the fat content the better, as this will prevent the sauce from splitting)
2 teaspoons lemon juice
½ teaspoon honey
¼ teaspoon cayenne pepper
Dried chilli flakes, to sprinkle

Place the whole pepper on an open gas flame or beneath a grill, turning the pepper occasionally with tongs to make sure that the skin chars and turns black all over. Allow the pepper to cool, then quarter it, pull off the blackened skin, deseed and roughly chop it. Set aside. (If you are pushed for pepper prep time, skip this step and use one from a jar of roasted peppers in oil.)

Bring a pan of water to the boil and salt it really well before adding the pasta. Cook according to the instructions on the packet, or until al dente.

Meanwhile, make the *tyrokafteri* sauce: crumble the feta into a blender or a food processor. Add the chopped red pepper and the rest of the ingredients (apart from the chilli flakes) and process until combined. The finished sauce can be as chunky or as smooth as you like.

Drain the tagliatelle, reserving a small cup of the cooking liquid.

Return the cooked pasta to the pan and add the *tyrokafteri*. Toss together gently over a low heat, adding as much of the reserved cooking liquid as necessary to give you a sauce that silkily coats your tagliatelle. Sprinkle with chilli flakes before serving.

10

Dine in for One

You can put on a show to the outside world,
but at what price inside?

This story is not just about food. It's about M&S food.
And my patient Polly.

Polly was one of the first patients I saw after I finished
my training. At the time, I had just joined a therapy clinic
near central London in an attempt to get my practice going.
There were lots of therapists renting rooms at this place,
so as the newbie I didn't have many slots to choose from.
The only after-work session available in the timetable was
Friday at 7 p.m. When I initially told Polly this was the
only time I could offer, I half expected her to turn it down,
because therapy isn't most people's idea of going out on a
Friday night. But Polly took up the slot without hesitation.

I should also add that there was an M&S Simply Food
opposite the practice.

Polly loved M&S food. The evidence was there in every
session: two bottle-green M&S bags would accompany Polly
into the therapy room, and the bags were always packed
liked sardines. There was always something similar about

the food items in both of her full-to-the-brim bags: they were cut-price products. Most of the items I saw were decorated with school-bus yellow stickers with bold black writing, indicating what 'WAS' and what was 'NOW', like someone was shouting the reduced price in your face. I have to say, it looked like Polly made some big savings on some very nice food, which once included my favourite: a pack of two Melt-in-the-Middle Chocolate Puddings (was £4, now £2). After a while, I started to wonder if M&S was part of the reason Polly was so keen to come to therapy at that time.

One day, I asked Polly about what looked like a very long-term relationship between her and M&S.

There was magic and sparkle in her voice as she spoke.

Polly waxed lyrical about the savings she would make by going to M&S after 5 p.m. I was impressed by how knowledgeable she was. According to Polly, the mid-afternoon reductions 'meant for mums on the school-run' were not nearly as good (only around 30 per cent), whereas after 5 p.m. items were reduced by up to 90 per cent. I had noticed money was a theme in Polly's story-telling. She spoke a lot about saving and 'not over-spending' and having 'expensive guilty pleasures' (only M&S, as far as I knew). I wasn't quite sure what she was squirrelling money away for; her salary as a senior civil servant was way above average.

But Polly didn't only love M&S yellow sticker food. She was completely enamoured by something else that was specific to M&S: the Dine In for Two for £10 deal.

This time she wanted to show me.

Polly rustled down into her bags and pulled out a vacuum-pack of two sirloin steaks (I could see they had heart-shaped pats of butter on top). 'This is the offer: see, you get a main, a side, a dessert and a bottle of wine for only a tenner! I get the offer every time it's on. So, I've got this as the main, and then chunky chips to go with it. And crème brûlées. The other time I got a whole rotisserie chicken. It's amazing, such a bargain!' said Polly. 'Normally this food would cost a king's ransom.' My father also uses that metaphor a lot, but he says 'the king's ransom', as if there has only ever been one king, and he usually throws in some profanity before either noun, which Polly didn't do. Still, she did speak like someone who was filled with joy about a grand event, like a royal wedding.

'Uh huh,' I said, urging her to continue. I was curious to see where Polly was going.

'Not that I've got anybody to dine in for two with,' she said, her smile fading. This was the unjoyful place Polly often got to. She didn't want M&S to be the only significant relationship in her life. Polly longed for a partner, and told me so in some way every session. Her fortieth birthday wasn't far away, and the fact that all of her close friends were now in twos, or threes or fours with families of their own made Polly yearn for someone special even more.

Polly seemed keen to continue our Dine In for Two conversation that session. But there was something a little monologue-like about it.

'Don't you see why I do it?' she asked, as if there was some obvious object in the room that I wasn't seeing.

'Do what?' I said.

'The deal,' Polly said.

'Do you mean the M&S deal?' I said.

'Yes, of course that's what I mean!' Polly held her hands up at me like an exasperated mother. 'Look, if I buy for two, then people will never know.'

'Which people will never know?' I said, bracing myself for round two of 'I know that you know that I know that you know'. Which I didn't, by the way.

'The checkout people,' said Polly.

'The checkout people will never know what?' I said.

Polly ignored my question. This wasn't unusual. Our dialogue was more like two monologues that happened to bump into each other every so often. She would speak in half sentences and expect me to just know the whole story. I now found myself mono-logging in my mind what I already knew about Polly, trying to work out what had previously passed me by about checkout people. As I attempted to keep up, Polly went on, like a speedy conveyor belt.

'It's the same with Mr Lam, when I place my order,' said Polly.

'What is?' I said. As my curiosity increased, so did her frustration. She flushed red.

'Gosh, Andrea, it's not rocket science! If I buy Dine In for Two, then the checkout person will think I'm part of a two. If I tell Mr Lam on the phone that I want the Shanghai Set Menu for Two, he'll think it's for a couple.' Polly widened her eyes and raised her brows, as though she was saying 'duh'. She didn't hide her disappointment that I wasn't following her basic meal-deal maths: buying dinner for two = one happy couple façade.

Polly was carefully crafting not just her dine-in menu, but herself. Having a fake dining partner was part of her false self, a defence designed to protect her true self inside, who was unhappy, single and dined in alone. She felt empty, so she filled herself up by buying food for two (although she was so slim, I wondered if she actually ate it all). To the outside world it looked like she had it all: Polly was pretty, popular and had a list of achievements as long as my arm. But these were all surface things. Her true feelings underneath were being covered up, not only in M&S, but here with me. In our sessions, Polly would try to be funny, which Freud would say was about anxiety or aggression; one of those feelings is always at the heart of any joke. Her anxiety about whether she was wanted and loveable came out in statements like: 'God, I sound like such a sad and stupid loner! Who would want to be with me?'

Sometimes she answered that question herself, with something along the lines of: 'Except you, Andrea. But you're just here because you're paid to be here.'

That was her aggression.

Polly often made comments about paying me. Unlike her M&S items, I didn't come with a cut-price yellow sticker.

Polly's reduced food items and Dine In for Two meals were for eating at the weekend. Polly had a lot of colleagues and friends, so she would frequently go out for weekday lunches and dinners. She rarely dined on her own during the week, and she cooked even less often than she ate alone.

'I don't cook, really,' said Polly. 'I will buy fruit and veg sometimes. Like if I fancy an apple, or for the odd time I'm not eating out, I'll microwave a potato or I'll just have carrot sticks with a pot of hummus. But I buy those in twos, too. I'd rather die than be seen buying one single carrot. I'd look like a right nobody.'

It could have almost been a song: 'The vegetables went in two by two'. But there was no 'hurrah' for Polly in any of this. She needed a fake Dine-In-for-Two somebody because otherwise she would be a real nobody. It was clear that she disagreed with Delia Smith's idea that 'One is Fun'. It was hard to imagine Polly, like Nigella Lawson, eating alone in a fairy-lit garden with an instrumental Paolo Nutini soundtrack playing in the background and feeling soothed and happy. That's because what Delia and Nigella enjoy is something psychologists call 'aloneliness'. It's a new concept that reflects how you can feel dissatisfied when your personal need for solitude is not met – when you want to spend more time alone than you typically do. This was not Polly, especially at the weekend. Once she said, 'You know, you're the only person I speak to from now until Monday.' (She immediately followed that with, 'God, how tragic is that! And you're paid to be here'). Because Saturdays and Sundays felt so long for her, she would eat dinner early, around 4 p.m. As she said, 'If you eat dinner, it means the day is over'. Polly didn't like dining alone at the table, so she ate in front of the television 'for company'.

Polly wasn't alonely. But she was a lonely person.

Loneliness is not just one thing. There are important differences between being alone and feeling alone. How many people you have around you does not necessarily add up to how connected or separated you feel. Polly described herself as a 'loner', though this wasn't true; most of the week she was with someone. She wasn't what psychologists call socially lonely. The problem for Polly was that one plus one big social circle wasn't equal to the feelings of attachment she wanted. Polly was emotionally lonely.

This idea of two types of loneliness is influenced by attachment theory. For emotionally lonely people, friendships supplement, but do not substitute for, an intimate partnership in staving off loneliness. What Polly wanted was a partner to fill-in for the attachment figure she hadn't had as a child and the feeling she had as a result. Emotional loneliness as an adult is a form of separation anxiety – it's the longing, the pining, the yearning for someone, one to one. It's your mind's way of trying to 'fix' the separation. Bowlby said it's this anxiety and painfulness of yearning that makes you repress your true self. This was something I had seen with my own eyes in my research on repression, attachment and stress. People who repress put up a front, especially in a social setting, where they will put on whatever face they think is desirable. They conceal, they don't feel. But Polly, like all lonely people, felt a lot. Loneliness has a lot of company; it sits with all the self-conscious emotions, like embarrassment, shyness, shame and guilt. Polly was trying to defend against all of these feelings with her cover-ups.

But there was one thing Polly made no pretence of, and it was the reason why she never cooked for one, or two, or any number of people: she couldn't cook. However, here was the culinary contradiction. Her mother was a cookery teacher and worked in a catering college; she taught everyone to cook apart from Polly. Her mother maintained that Polly 'was never interested' in cooking when she was growing up, but I wondered if that was a cover-up story her mother had told herself. It didn't sound like Polly's mother was interested in spending any time with her at all, even when she was a child. Polly's mother was 'always stressed', either with work or because of taking Polly to her numerous extra-curricular activities. Polly, in her words, 'did it all': every day of the week there was something, whether it was singing, dancing, piano, violin, archery, athletics, gymnastics, German or French. Really, Polly didn't want to do so much, but she dare not tell her mother for fear of upsetting her or appearing ungrateful. She said her mother 'spent an arm and a leg' on all her activities.

The only one-to-one time Polly spent with her mother was on a Saturday morning, when the two of them would go to M&S (or St. Michael, as it was known then). After they had finished their shopping in the food hall, they would go to the café together. Before they ordered, Polly's mother would ask her about whatever test, competition, grading, race or assessment was happening at the time. The rule was that Polly could only have a cake if she had 'done well enough'. If not, she could only have a drink. Polly said she struggled to keep up with school and all her activities, so there were several times she was left out while her mother dined in with cake for one at the M&S café. Sometimes Polly would make up her grades so that she could have cake too. Polly had learned to present her false self in M&S from a young age, and this persona was the hidden price she had paid for her mother's approval. Everything was about serving her mother's needs; Polly's needs or wants were never seen. She didn't even get to choose which cake she had. Polly was related to as an object – a human doing rather than a human being. I could see why she felt like a nobody.

You become a 'somebody' in an attachment relationship. Having a loved one tune into you emotionally is how you discover yourself as a real, true psychological somebody, with needs and wants. It made sense that Polly's need for me to read her mind almost felt narcissistic sometimes; if you haven't been seen, then you look for mirrors. Polly had never had the experience of someone tuning into how she felt. She was only ever noticed for what she did – for what was on show. So this was what she did: she put on a show. This was what Polly's parents did too. Their friends and family still saw them as the 'happy couple' after fifty years. I didn't get the impression that Polly's parents were happy, much less that they were a couple. There was no emotion on show, now or then. Growing up, Polly's parents were never affectionate towards each other, or argumentative either. No kisses or conflict or anything in between. They didn't do feelings, seemingly. They didn't do a lot as a couple at all, other than dine out together sometimes, and that was always with friends. They would also go on holiday with friends twice a year to 'posh places'. That was the extent of their togetherness. Now that Polly's parents were retired, most of their time was spent on extra-marital activities (her mother now spent all day in the garden instead of the kitchen). They seemed to stay together by being separate.

This was Polly's recipe for a relationship: a partner was something to have, literally, as an object, not a person to hold in mind with love – or attach to. I could now see through Polly's yellow-sticker shopping and other money-saving behaviour: she was trying to take care of her own security because she'd never learned that anyone could really be there for her. The fake Dine In partner was just another way of covering up and denying a real attachment need for a someone to depend on.

There came a time, though, when the feelings underneath Polly's cover-up caught up with her – and it happened in M&S. One day, after about a year of working together, Polly arrived for our Friday night session exactly on time, as usual. Although she looked the same, there was something different about her. She walked in, stomping her ballet flats on the floor in a way that didn't feel like her typically poised, balletic self. After we sat down, I realised Polly didn't have any M&S bags with her.

This was a first.

I pointed this out to her.

'I didn't go. I went on Sunday. I'm not going back,' she said, like it was a done deal.

She seemed to close down as we sat in silence for a moment.

Then I remembered: Sunday was Valentine's Day.

When Polly chose to open up our conversation again, her topic of choice was not the warm fuzziness of flowers and chocolates and teddy bears. She wanted to talk cold, hard cash.

'They overcharged me,' said Polly.

'Who did?' I said.

'M&S did! It's a bloody travesty. Honestly, it's not like they don't get enough out of me,' said Polly, looking right at me.

Polly then went on to tell me about the travesty that had happened. It involved the Dine In for Two deal, which this time was £20 instead of £10, because the Valentine's version came with 'more posh options', as well as pink fizz and chocolates. Polly had been especially excited about what was on offer. She had spent time in the aisles, choosing what she wanted for her starter (two smoked salmon mousse 'pearls'), main course (two fillet of beef wellington), side (garlic mushrooms) and dessert (two tiramisus).

So far, so usual.

Polly had even gone to her usual checkout person: Reg. They only ever said two words to one another, which were 'hello' and 'thanks'. After greeting each other, Reg proceeded to scan Polly's items. When he finished, he told her the total price of her shopping: £36.75.

Polly, who was standing with her £20 note at the ready, asked Reg what was wrong.

'I'm sorry, Miss, you haven't got the correct dessert for the Valentine's Day Dine In for Two. I'm afraid the pack of two tiramisus isn't included in the deal,' said Reg. 'The good news is that if you like Italian, you could get the two raspberry panna cottas. Or go French with the two tarte au citron slices. The wife says they're lovely, very lemony. Why don't you go and get that instead? Just a quick swap and the deal will go through. Easy peasy lemon squeezy, as they say.'

This wasn't good news for Polly. It also wasn't that easy. She wasn't used to getting things wrong. Especially in M&S.

'I'm sure the tiramisus are part of the deal. I'm in here often. I do know.' Polly glared at Reg.

'I know, Miss, I recognise you. You come in on your own usually on a Friday evening,' said Reg, nodding.

The recognition was too much for Polly. And so was the possibility that Reg had seen through her Dine In defence.

First, she went red.

Then, she saw red. Not Valentine's hearts and roses red. More like red mist.

'Excuse me, why do you keep presuming I'm Miss? Maybe I might be married and I'm Mrs, for all you know,' said Polly. There was no sparkle in her voice.

'I'm sorry, love, I didn't know. As I said, if you go back and choose one of the other desserts, I'll put the deal through for you. I don't want you and your fella to miss out on the saving,' said Reg.

It didn't matter what Reg said. Deal or no deal, Polly now couldn't see through the red mist. If she could, she would have seen that Reg was no longer nodding his head. Instead, his hands were shaking as they held the double pack of tiramisus. Polly was now blind with rage.

'Don't you talk about my fucking fella!' shouted Polly.

Suddenly, as if by magic, all of M&S stopped talking.

The other couples queuing at the checkout forgot about their heart-shaped punnets of strawberries for choco-late dipping, and whatever else was on the menu later. All eyes were now on Polly and Reg as the temperature rose between them, in a very un-Valentine's way. Reg was silent, and Polly was shouting for two.

The security guard came over and asked if everything was all right. At that point, Polly burst into tears and ran out of the shop, leaving her Dine In deal behind. She sat in her car, there in the M&S carpark, and sobbed non-stop for twenty minutes.

This was not just a meltdown. This was an M&S meltdown.

Polly had spent a lifetime skating on top of her emotional world and now it was starting to unfreeze. Her defence was breaking down, or at least it was in M&S. Here with me, she couldn't seem to let it go. Having told me the story, she was back to controlled and poised Polly.

'I'm wondering what's occurring for you now, Polly,' I said.

'Nothing,' said Polly, giving an indifferent shrug. 'It's all worked out okay. The food's overpriced and I'm wasting my money because I don't eat all of it anyway. To be fair, I'm spending far too much every month, what with paying you. It's a lot for a single person to manage on their own.'

We were back to the non-cut-price therapy comments.

I wasn't going to paper over (or put a yellow sticker on) what Polly had said.

'Maybe I'm like M&S: I also charge you. I wonder how that feels for you,' I said.

Polly quickly used her customary defence.

'You're paid to be here,' she said, her eyes holding me at a distance.

I took a moment to hold her gaze. Then I replied using my true self.

'Yes, I have needs too, some of which are taken care of by the fee. I need to make a living, I can't cover that up,' I said. 'But that doesn't mean I don't have a need for

meaningful work, or that I don't truly want to help you.'
I was a somebody, trying to let Polly know that I saw her
as a somebody too.

'But this is a business interaction,' said Polly, in a corpo-
rate tone to match her statement.

'Maybe it feels safer to think of therapy like that. And of
me as just this distant, two-dimensional transaction, rather
than a real person with whom you interact in a real way.
Because then you won't get close, or risk depending on me.
And if that's the case, then you won't get disappointed or
rejected or hurt. Perhaps, in a way, I'm like your fake Dine
In for Two partner,' I said.

Polly was quiet. Not Reg-stunned-in-M&S silent, but
thoughtfully quiet. I wondered if something was starting
to sink in.

Then I said something else that was true.

'In therapy, the interaction – the relationship – isn't pretend. It's real, Polly,' I said. 'So, to borrow your word, the
"business" is personal, in a sense: it's a relationship, and
like any other, it must work for two people. We are both
choosing to work together. And what goes on in the relationship between me and you, here and now, those feelings might feel familiar to you. That's the real way therapy
works. And we can talk about this,' I said.

So we did.

For the first time, Polly and I had a conversation about us.

That was the day Polly broke up with her fake Dine In
for Two relationship.

But it was also the day the therapy became more of a real relationship for two.

* * *

Lemon Mahalebi Tart

This is my tribute to the tarte au citron that Reg in M&S suggested Polly should buy for the Valentine's Dine In for Two deal. I, however, haven't gone French; I've gone Greek with my version. A classic lemon tart contains double cream, but here I've halved the work by using a mahalebi-style filling. (Mahalebi is a traditional Cypriot custard-like dessert made with cornflour, milk and sugar.) Easy peasy lemon squeezy, as they say.

Serves 8

For the pastry:
150g plain flour
Pinch of salt
85g chilled butter
2 tablespoons caster sugar
25g ground almonds
1 egg yolk

For the lemon mahalebi filling:
3 lemons
3 tablespoons cornflour
600ml milk
3 tablespoons caster sugar

Sift the flour into a bowl and add the salt. Cut the butter into small pieces and add it to the flour. Take two cutlery knives and 'cut' the butter into the flour – try to mimic a scissor action. Using knives instead of your fingers is helpful for keeping everything cool.

Once the butter has been cut down to pea-sized pieces, use your fingertips to gently, but quickly, rub the butter into the flour until you have a mixture that resembles fine, pale breadcrumbs, with no large lumps of butter remaining.

Stir the sugar and ground almonds into the flour-and-butter crumb.

Whisk the egg yolk with 2 tablespoons of water in a small bowl. Using a cutlery knife, stir in a couple of tablespoons of the yolk mixture into the crumb mixture – you will see it start to turn into large flakes. Add just enough liquid to bind it. Use the flat of your knife to press together the large flakes and the dry crumb, then pull the pastry together with your hands. Remove the pastry from the bowl and on a clean work surface shape it into a flat disc, a couple of centimetres thick. Wrap the pastry in cling film and chill for 20–30 minutes before rolling out.

When you are ready to bake the pastry, preheat the oven to 200°C/180°C fan/gas mark 6. Flour both your work surface and your rolling pin. Roll the pastry into a circle large enough to line the bottom and sides of a 20cm pie tin – the pastry will be around 3mm thick. The best way to line the tin is to carefully wrap the pastry circle over the rolling pin and unfold it gently over the pie tin. Ease the pastry into the nooks and crannies of the tin, ensuring the dough is smoothed up the sides. Take your rolling pin and roll over the top to remove the excess pastry. Use the leftover pastry to patch up any holes.

Take a piece of baking parchment larger than the tin and scrunch it up. Unfold it and place on top of the pastry. Add a layer of baking beans (these are ceramic beans for blind-baking pastry; if you don't have any, you could use dried beans) and fold any excess paper over the sides of the tin. Bake the pastry case in the oven for 15–20 minutes.

After this time the sides will have set and become slightly golden. Carefully remove the paper and the beans and return the pastry case to the oven for a further 5–10 minutes. When the pastry case is ready, the base will be dry and sandy to the touch and the edges will be biscuit-coloured. Remove from the oven and allow to cool while you make the filling.

To make the mahalebi, first zest the lemons. Mix together the cornflour with a small cup of the milk until smooth. Place the remaining milk in a saucepan together with the sugar. Warm over medium-low heat until the milk is scalded. Pour in the cornflour mixture and whisk continuously for 4–5 minutes, or until the mahalebi has the consistency of thick custard. Remove the saucepan from the heat and stir in the lemon zest.

Pour the mahalebi into the pastry case. Leave to cool, then refrigerate until you are ready to eat. Serve with fresh berries.

Part III

LOSS

Once Upon a Table, There Was Spaghetti

Can you find love in loss?

This begins like a lot of other food stories: I am standing in my kitchen and I am cooking.

An obvious first line for a food story, I know. Apart from my grandmother in Cyprus, I don't know many people who cook sitting down. She would often sit on a chair in the garden, beneath a trellis abundant with bougainvillea and vines, and cook on a little gas hob. My grandmother would also sit to chop her vegetables; she would cradle them in her lap, taking each one into her hand to chop it in mid-air with her melamine-handled table knife. The blade had the softest serrations, like baby teeth marks. I don't chop like my grandmother, but I do have a similar knife — it's the one I'm using now.

I am cooking dinner for me and my boyfriend, Bruno. I hate using the word 'boyfriend'; it feels so young, like we're teenagers. But we're not. We're in our twenties. Bruno is in the living area next door, tucked up on the bean bag arm-chair. He wears a *Fast and Furious* t-shirt. We went to see that film together a few years ago on our first date. I remember how Bruno's hair had that perfectly gelled boy-band look. It still does. Bruno, at this moment, is deeply engrossed in whatever he is looking at on his iPad. We will have dinner together this evening, but it doesn't feel like a date.

I am standing in the kitchen and I am cooking a tomato sauce for dinner tonight, which I will serve with spaghetti. Earlier today, on the way back from the hospital, I picked up some tomatoes from Waitrose, which remind me of the ones my grandmother used to grow in her garden: they are perfectly red and rounded with just the right amount of squish, like a baby's bottom. I chop the tomatoes into random shapes and sizes that look as though they belong to a child's shape-sorter toy. As I stand at the counter chopping, a question comes to mind: why don't tomatoes bleed? Their raw redness makes it look like they ought to be oozing thick blood from that deep, first cut. Instead, they seep. Insipidly. The tomato wounds cause watery dribble all over my chopping board. And now, for some reason, I can also feel water dribbling out of my eyes. Little droplets move slowly down my face and join up under my chin. I am not crying, though. There is nothing to cry about – and I am no cry baby. These are just crocodile tears. Or onion tears. Yes, that's what they are, because I cut the onions first, before the tomatoes. Of course, the onions have inflicted tears on me because I attacked them. It's my fault. I cut them and I hurt them. Just now I heard the onions wail as they hit the hot pan. I'm sorry. I empathise. Because

I have tears too. Maybe tomatoes and onions contain the same chemical that makes you cry? Someone should research that question. At the same time, they could find an answer to the more important question of why these tomatoes, right now – actually, why *all* tomatoes – have fake wounds. They look like they should bleed. Why are they not bleeding?

Because I am.

I am standing in the kitchen, I am cooking dinner and I am bleeding.

Because I am losing my baby.

***

The night I lost my baby, I was looking for a safe haven. So I cooked something that was comforting and familiar and associated with someone who made me feel safe and sound as a child. I wanted the retro warmth of my mother's 1980s kitchen with its lino and Formica, and I wanted the spaghetti with tomato sauce that she would cook for me on her freestanding Cannon gas cooker. My mother's tomato sauce had special Cypriot touches: she'd throw in a stick of cinnamon and a smattering of dried mint for sweetness. The key ingredient in my mother's sauce, however, was not the cinnamon or the mint, nor the tomatoes or the olive oil: it was time. The sauce was quick and easy to prepare, so cooking time didn't eat into 'just us' time too much. At the table, she would cut up my spaghetti into what looked like offcuts from my Play-Doh Mop Top Hair toy, which were perfect for me to teaspoon into my mouth. There was no long strand of pasta to connect us or meatballs, like the iconic spaghetti scene in *Lady and the Tramp*, but those suppers still had a Disney-like magic to them. And the dish has endured: it is the (spaghetti) tie that binds us, exactly as Ainsworth meant when she said attachments bridge gaps in time and space. I mentioned Mum Food in earlier chapters. This is mine.

There were actually meant to be meatballs that night. On the way home, I had also bought sausages to make Nigella's Shortcut Sausage Meatballs. But as dinner time neared, I did an unconscious U-turn. Suffice to say, spaghetti with meatballs was not my comfort food. The other problem was the episode of *Nigellissima* that featured the recipe showed her very much in Italian mama mode, making the dish with her niece and nephew. She said small people with small hands were better-suited to rolling the cherry tomato-sized meatballs. The comment rolled around in my mind. Now, for me and Bruno, there would be no small person with small hands, no pitter-patter of tiny feet. My pregnancy, from start to finish, felt like a series of unfortunate events: one, the coil I'd had fitted quickly uncoiled itself from my womb and I got pregnant immediately with it still inside me; two, I hadn't realised I was pregnant for a few weeks, and then lost the baby only a week after I'd found out; and three, Bruno had recoiled at the idea of being a father. He had always said he didn't want children, which was the most unfortunate and painful part of the story. Perhaps it was even more unfortunate that I went along with the relationship knowing that, and hoping that some day he would change his mind.

As I lost my baby, my food of love became the food of loss. That night, over our dinner of spaghetti and tomato sauce, Bruno and I unconsciously uncoupled. We sat at our table, eating together in silence. It was clear that something more had been lost than just our baby. Our relationship already had emotional cracks, which words fell into because they went unsaid. Neither of us had felt safe or satisfied for a long time. Too long. I felt disconnected, both from Bruno and from the food in front of me. Not only was I miscarrying, I was mis-cooking. The tomato sauce had a tinny tang to it and tasted like I'd licked an unlucky penny. At the last minute, I tried to fix it by squirting in some ketchup; the gobs clotted on the surface of the sauce. Then I overcooked the spaghetti, so it was even more swollen than I was; it congealed and clumped together in the pot. It was all just disgusting.

On the saddest night of my life, I went looking for feelings of soothing spaghetti dinners past, but I didn't find them on my plate, or in Bruno, who became deafer to my needs as the evening went on. I apologised to him for how shit the dinner was and went to bed early, alone. I scrunched myself into a foetal position on our bed, dizzy with the punching pain of the cramps. I desperately wanted the discomfort to go away. But there was something else I wanted more. I had a longing that was deep and unyielding, that I didn't want to say out loud because Bruno was within earshot. The secret words felt like lumps in my throat. I tried to bargain with myself: *say whatever you like. Scream, swear, shout song lyrics. Anything. Just don't say those words*. Me saying those words would be like sticking a knife in a soufflé. It would be the undoing of our relationship, the point of emotional no return. The words became louder; each one was like a pang of raw feeling. Then it happened. I stopped hearing myself and I started listening to myself. As a small puddle formed on my pillow, all fight left my body. I let the words, like the tears, fall out of me: 'I want my mum.'

I didn't just want my mother's spaghetti with tomato sauce. I wanted my mother, my original attachment figure. Bruno wasn't my special person anymore; I had lost my safe haven in him.

Loss and separation is where attachment theory first started, and Bowlby looked at the effects of this in children. At that time, mother–child separation was often considered maternal deprivation. Although Winnicott is most famous for his concept of the 'good-enough' mother, he made an important contribution to Bowlby's early ideas by explaining the difference between deprivation and privation. Deprivation is the breaking of a bond, whereas privation is the non-making of a bond. So deprivation = loss, privation = never had.

In the aftermath of my miscarriage, I could relate to both: maternal deprivation and privation. I lost something I never had. The thing is, it felt like I did have something – or someone. From the beginning, my baby had had a place not only in my heart, but in my home. The day I discovered I was pregnant, I wandered into the baby aisle in Waitrose and ended up buying Farley's rusks. The day after that, I was browsing in Robert Dyas and bought a set of Tupperware, perfect for holding dinky amounts of puréed veg. Less than a week later, I was pottering around the kitchen and found myself wondering if my mother had kept my Bunnykins bowl; I didn't know that would be the last day of my pregnancy.

I felt like a childless mother.

When a mother–baby bond isn't made, as is the case with privation, Winnicott said that this is because of a failure in the 'facilitating environment'. He didn't mean environment literally, even though I took it that way. Bowlby said that in this context, by environment Winnicott seemed to mean mother. That didn't make me feel any better. I will never know the reason why I miscarried. But what remains in my memory from the blur of countless conversations with doctors is something about the failure of my internal environment: my 'inhospitable uterus'. I was left feeling as though if I had just bought the right soft furnishings from Ikea to make my womb welcoming and cosy it would all have been okay. Inhospitable. Really? For fuck's sake, I'm Greek. The Greeks *invented* hospitality.

I later found out that Ainsworth's only pregnancy resulted in a miscarriage. But she didn't work through her feelings about the loss of her baby until another loss happened a little later on. When her marriage ended, Ainsworth chose therapy to help with her unhappiness (she later described her experience of therapy as the most important positive influence on her career). Whereas when I miscarried and my relationship was breaking down, I chose to cook my version of what Laurie Colwin calls 'edible therapy' to help things feel better. Really, though, there was no dish that was going to heal the rupture in my relationship with Bruno. The loss of the baby was the spaghetto that broke the camel's back. At the start of Ainsworth's eight years in therapy, she struggled to feel any anger, and just felt hurt. She later realised how furious she was. I, however, had no such problem with repressed anger. I fully expressed my anger and entwined it into every interaction Bruno and I had. We couldn't talk, so we argued. And then arguing became the easy way of saying all the things we couldn't talk about. And then arguing became the only way of talking. But talking was the only thing that was going to help me with my feelings. *Real* talking. I mean real therapy, not just edible therapy.

Unlike Ainsworth, I didn't have to find a therapist. Luckily, I already had one in my life – the same person I still see now. She is called Delia. Coincidence, I know, given that this is a food book. But her surname is not Smith, and we were working together long before this book was born, for about a year before Bruno and I started dating. It was my many experiences of lost, unrequited and unhappily-ever-after romantic love that prompted me to go to therapy. As time went by, we naturally progressed to the typical therapeutic exploration of how your parents fuck you up, and how to reconcile my feelings about the fact that they didn't mean to.

When I was looking for a psychoanalyst, Delia's name was probably part of the reason I was drawn to her; the only other person I had ever known with that name was the iconic 1990s television cook. But now, if the name Delia was mentioned to me in a word-association test (the kind that therapists love), my Delia would be the first one who comes to mind. I have never seen my Delia's kitchen; I don't know if she has a big lazy Susan table, like Delia Smith. She has a lot of books, though. My Delia would say that the answers to all life's problems lie in literary classics, rather than in teaching people to cook. For a long time, I didn't know anything about her cooking capacity. But after a couple of years of working together I did ask her if she knew how to cook, and if she owned a copy of Delia (Smith)'s *How to Cook*. Her answers were 'not really' and 'no', respectively. I think my Delia enjoys eating, but I'm not sure how much she cares for cooking. She does, however, care for me. She sits with me, week in week out, thinking and talking about my life, psychologically holding my hand and figuratively catching my tears (she has the largest hands I have ever seen on a woman). Delia Smith may have an effect on the public when she uses specific ingredients and utensils (when she recommended a lemon zester there was a national shortage), but as far as I'm concerned, the real Delia effect is therapeutic.

**

Looking back, it was all in the food. There were gastronomical nuances at the start of my relationship with Bruno that warned me this was not going to end happily ever after. I sometimes kick myself for not having paid closer attention at the time, but hindsight (and a lot of therapy) is a wonderful thing. Love blinds your palate as well as your eyes.

The first thing: I never used to eat cheese. I would sometimes have halloumi in certain dishes my mother made and I would eat cheese and onion crisps, but that was about it. (I have slightly broadened my cheese horizons in recent years.) Yet on our first date I copied Bruno at the restaurant and ordered the five-cheese risotto: a big, gelatinous blob oozing with mozzarella, mascarpone, gorgonzola, fontina and taleggio. I wanted to show Bruno that I was just like him and we had the same taste, and I was therefore loveable. Nauseous was what I was – and deluded. After we said goodbye, I went to Tesco Express on my way home and bought a cut-priced yellow-stickered tub of watermelon cubes to cleanse my palate. The fact that I made a beeline for something that would save me a few pennies was indicative that I didn't feel secure.

Another thing: we had significant coffee differences. Bruno's coffee was long and milky, while mine was short, strong and black as night. Bruno also loved Starbucks, whereas I'm not a fan of their coffee in any way, shape or form. I like a blended word as much as anyone else, but 'Frappuccino' really grinds me. Just call a cold coffee what it is: a frappé. Have you seen their most recent range? It's called Oleato and it's infused with extra virgin olive oil. I love olive oil, but I draw the line at adding it to my coffee.

And another thing: we had a culture clash when it came to mash. Bruno's heritage was a mix of western and northern European (the biggest part of him was German, a miniscule part of him was French, a small part was Scandinavian and a tiny part was from Jersey). He may have been split across several countries but there was enough butter in all of those cuisines to emulsify him. Butter is what went into Bruno's mashed potatoes (or his *Kartoffelstampf*). Loads of it. The ancient Greeks used to insult northern Europeans by calling them 'butter eaters', but that is what Bruno was. To this day, I wonder if he found my copy of *Heartburn* and copied Nora Ephron's recipe: Bruno added as much melted butter as he felt like, and most of the time there was more butter than potatoes in his mashed potatoes. I do agree with Nora that there is nothing like mashed potatoes when you're feeling blue, but the butter is where she and I part ways. In my opinion, the secret to making good mash is not only Cyprus potatoes, but lashings of extra virgin olive oil and, of course, salt. No pepper, because that's the job of the olive oil. The best break-up food in the world is a bowl of hot mashed potatoes dressed with chilled olive oil, salt and a spritz of lemon: it will fool you into thinking you are sitting in the sunshine at a whitewashed taverna by the sea, when really your heart is cold and breaking.

One more thing: Bruno was a big meat-eater, whereas a natural vegan diet is common for Greek Cypriots, and what I preferred. At the time, the Byron restaurant franchise was popular on the posh burger scene and it was Bruno's favourite place to eat, so we went there a lot during our relationship. For me, the best thing on the menu were the courgette fries.

But in terms of food forebodings, there was one thing so big and so significant that it should have been the most obvious warning sign. It practically came with a neon arrow pointing at it. Are you ready for it? He would cut his burger in quarters. In quarters! I mean, really? It was as though he couldn't bring himself to commit to the all-in hand-hugging that a whole burger hold requires. I should have known from the start that he had a commitment problem and intimacy issues.

***

The time eventually came to move out and move on, in our individual ways. Bruno and I didn't stay friends, but after we handed back the keys to the flat we did stay in touch for a little while. I noticed during those weeks that Bruno put on a lot of weight (remember *Kummerspeck* from Chapter 4: 'grief bacon'). He was clearly working his way through a lot of bacon, burgers and emotions. Bruno asked me for help finding a therapist, a question which I took to my Delia. She referred him to a colleague. Although Bruno wasn't the love rat *Heartburn's* Mark was, they both had the same problem when it came to paying for therapy: stinginess. Bruno asked me if the therapist would offer a discount because of the link to Delia. I said I was doubtful that the person's fee schedule would include a 'therapeutic family rate'. Given his obsession with quarters, Bruno probably asked for a fourth off the price anyway.

After it was over, I discovered I had a problem: I didn't want to talk about it. By 'it' I meant both my miscarriage and my break-up with Bruno. I couldn't bring myself to go there. Deep down, I knew why. There was one thought that whirred around in my mind like an ambulance siren: *this is going to hurt.*

But I was wrong: this had already hurt.

I had lost my baby and I had lost Bruno. The events, the stress, the trauma, had happened already. What hadn't happened was me exploring or experiencing the feelings underneath, because I was terrified that talking about the pain would somehow make it more painful. But the reality was that I didn't have to sit alone with the pain; there was someone I could take it to, who could hold it. You can take risks in safe hands. With my Delia by my side, slowly, session by session, I allowed myself to, in Winnicott's words, 'breakdown', or rather, break free from what was hiding beneath all the anger I felt. I wasn't so different from Ainsworth after all: I found my hurt. And surely, as I did, I found out what my own lifelong model of love was: that love hurts. That was my recipe for relationships. Professionally, I had spent the last decade researching and promoting attachment theory. Personally, I was a textbook case of imposter syndrome. I had no faith in attachment. In my life's experience, relationships were just things that left you head to toe with disappointment, weight on your shoulders and knees knocking with unease. That all changed when I was pregnant. It was a chance to right all past relational wrongs. It felt magical, like me as a child using the eraser bar to wipe clean my Magna Doodle. Me and my baby were a twosome. This couple, our couple, was one I could trust. My love for this baby was alive and kicking from day one. It was like I was born, this whole part of me I didn't know I had. Suddenly, I had all this love to give. A new love had found a home in me.

And then that love was homeless.

That was my grief. It had found me.

In some of those sessions with Delia it felt like I cried for 48 out of our 50 minutes together, barely leaving a minute each for hello and goodbye. The tears were eventually replaced with words. Then I talked like an open wound. Delia listened to it all. I mean really listened. She observed. She was patient. She validated my grief exactly. And not just about the baby.

Once summer arrived, about six months later, I had some different grieving to do in my work at university.

It's always bittersweet to say goodbye to students you've taught for several years. During one session with Delia, I was talking about a student I had grown quite fond of, a young woman who had transformed over the course of her degree to become confident and curious, a far cry from the gawky teenager I'd met three years earlier. After a small silence, Delia gazed softly at me and said in her classic Delia way, 'Sometimes watching a person grow psychologically is the closest experience to watching a beloved child change.'

I looked at Delia looking at me. That was the original light-bulb moment. Delia saw me as a mother. I guess that was Delia's 'throw-in', as Yalom would say; her added extra. She threw it into the therapy when no one was looking – I certainly wasn't. It was a very special ingredient that helped to rework my relationship recipe at that time.

Every day, I felt like I was getting a little closer to something. My heart felt like it was being reset or reorganised, or at least it felt a little less broken. The tiny little pieces of it were being put back together. The blood was starting to run through my maternal veins again. It was time to find a new home for all that love. So I decided to train to be a therapist. I applied to the psychotherapy training programme at the Bowlby Centre the following year. At the time, I told people it was because I was looking to add another string to my bow, to complete my holy work trinity of attachment theory teaching, research and now practice. But the truth was, it felt like the best way I could be a mother.

So my own food story ended up being happily ever after, in an unlikely way. That dish of spaghetti with tomato sauce, which has gone through the cycle of attachment, separation and loss, I now think of as being part of my journey back to love – a different kind of love from what I had expected. Freud said that psychotherapy is the work of love, and he was right. So was my mother when she said that things will work out for the best if you make the best of how they work out. For Nora Ephron, that involved con-verting her tragedy into a comedy – she said she knew the moment her marriage ended that someday it might make a book. I didn't. I'm sure Bruno never thought during any of the times when he was nibbling through the third quar-ter of his Byron cheeseburger that I would end up writ-ing about it in a book. Nora also said her mother taught her many things when she was growing up, but the main thing she learned from her is that everything is copy. Now I see just how right Nora's mother was. Everything is copy. Every single bite.

* * *

Spaghetti with Tomato Sauce

I still make this dish, and to this day it remains my Mum Food.

Serves 2

2 tablespoons olive oil
1 small onion, peeled and finely chopped

1 tablespoon tomato purée
6 tomatoes, chopped into small chunks
1 teaspoon dried mint
½ teaspoon salt
¼ teaspoon ground black pepper
1 small cinnamon stick
2 dried bay leaves
200g spaghetti
Grated halloumi, to serve

Heat the olive oil in a saucepan over medium heat. Add the onion and cook for a few minutes, until the pieces are a pale golden colour and softened. Add the tomato purée and cook, stirring, for a couple of minutes.

Add the chopped tomatoes to the pan and stir for a further minute. Mix in the dried mint, salt, pepper, cinnamon stick and bay leaves, then add about 75ml of water.

Bring to the boil, cover and simmer on a medium heat for about 10 minutes, or until the sauce has reduced and thickened. Bring a pan of water to the boil, salt generously and then add the spaghetti. Cook according to the instructions on the packet, or until al dente. Drain the spaghetti. To serve, put the spaghetti on a plate, ladle the tomato sauce on top (something I learned from my mother) and sprinkle with as much grated halloumi as you like.

12

McDonald's · Eat · Repeat

Is your relationship safe haven really a bunker?

'Every day?' I said.

'Every day,' my patient, Serge, repeated.

I'd never heard anything like that before. Ever.

'Every day for the past twenty years,' I said, trying to hide my surprise.

'Yeah,' Serge nodded.

I found myself mirroring Serge's nodding. I wasn't sure whether it was my shock reverberating around the room or the breeze from the fan that was causing the Freud bobblehead doll on my desk to do the same. Of course, Freud would be nodding; this was free association at its best. Free association, as you may remember from Chapter 6, is when a person says whatever is going through their mind. When Freud came up with this concept, he was referring to the patient's mind, not the therapist's. So naturally I didn't say what came into my head when Serge said what he said. But take it from me: I had a lot on my mind about it. So much so that I wanted to talk about it in my own therapy. I wondered what Delia (both mine and Smith, too, for that matter) would say about the fact that Serge had just told me that he'd eaten the same lunch every day for the past twenty years.

The thing I couldn't get my head around was that it didn't even sound like a very nice lunch. Every day, Serge would eat a chicken sandwich and a packet of cheese and onion crisps. By chicken sandwich, I don't mean softly juicy chunks of roasted chicken between two thick slices of a flour-dusted farmhouse loaf spread with mayonnaise, maybe also some lettuce and slices of vine-ripened tomatoes. Serge's sandwich was made with bog-standard sliced white bread, the stuff that is paradoxically plastic and spongy. The filling was – wait for it – wafer-thin chicken slices. You know, the stuff that looks and feels like (and probably tastes like) a cream-coloured shower curtain. This was what Serge had eaten for his lunch every day since he was ten years old. Reformed chicken had been the formative food in all his formative years, from childhood to adolescence and now adulthood. Nutritionally, I suppose at least it gave him some protein. But it certainly wasn't gastronomy. There was no pleasure in it either; I don't think Serge even liked his lunch that much, despite eating it every day. It's been said that eating is what a person does, appetite is what they feel. Serge didn't seem to feel, or think, a lot. In fact, that seemed to be the point of his chicken sandwich lunch: he said, 'It's quick, I don't have to think about it and it fills me up.' It was fast food, of sorts. However, it was the furthest thing from the crispy-coated, fast-food version of chicken I was more familiar with.

Incidentally, there is a great recipe for a fried chicken sandwich in Nigella Lawson's book, *Cook, Eat, Repeat*, which, in a way, is what this story is all about.

Serge hadn't come to therapy for help with his repetitive lunch (although I really felt the urge to help him with that). He'd come to therapy for help with his love life. How much love there was in his life, I wasn't sure. But there were certainly a lot of dates: Serge was a serial online dater, and would go out on several dates a week. Part of me was impressed, but those were just my own feelings I was transferring into the mix. As a therapist, dating is a bit of an occupational hazard. If I had a pound for every time a date has said to me, 'So, you're a therapist? Are you analysing me right now?' I'd be eating in Michelin-starred restaurants every night. A date has turned into a session far too many times than I care to admit. Still, it could be worse, particularly in the world of online dating, which is full of pitfalls: I have a colleague who is still trying to repair the most unfortunate Freudian-finger-slip left swipe on their patient.

Serge had done a lot of scrolling and swiping over the years. In our conversations about this, I had to remind myself that we were talking about dating, because Serge talked about his potential partners as though they were choices on a takeaway menu. He had a list of requirements. He wanted a woman who was attractive, funny, well-travelled and not too tall. She needed to have 'good chat' and 'not be boring' but not be 'too over the top'. When I asked him what he meant by that, he said: 'emotionally efficient'.

I felt like I was a waitress taking his order. 'Would you like fries with that?' was the expression that came to mind.

Actually, Serge did want fries with that. He loved a take-away too – but not just any takeaway. He wasn't going to patiently wait for some Zen sushi master to roll maki or slice sashimi. No, Serge liked the heated bustle of places that served hot fried food. About his fast-food preferences, he said: 'It's fast, I don't have to wait for it and it fills me up.' McDonald's was Serge's favourite, and he would visit the 24-hour one a few minutes from his house every week-end, without fail. He said he 'loved it'. Serge told me that last week during our second session: it was the first time he had used the word 'love'.

My mother loves McDonald's. It was her first fast-food love, and she was faithful until Charlie Bigham, with his range of hand-prepared ready meals, came on the scene in the 1990s; after that, she started spending more time at home with him. My father, however, has always been loyal to the place that gave him security when he came over after the war in Cyprus, his first secure base in the UK: Wimpy. The manager let my father live for free on top of the shop in exchange for working there. So for a short while my father had a West End pad and a career at the coolest restaurant in town. The menu was also pretty cos-mopolitan compared to McDonald's. I think the Wimpy International Grill helped my father to feel at home; to this day, the dish features a sausage that looks and tastes uncannily like a Greek *loukaniko* and the bun-less burger is basically a Greek *bifteki*. At the time, Wimpy was ahead of the dessert curve too. The only offering McDonald's had was the apple pie, which wasn't bad, although it barely had any apple in it. Wimpy's choice of desserts all came with the chain's very own soft-serve vanilla ice cream. My father was a Brown Derby man (the legendary Wimpy dessert that was the bargain price of 15p in 1974). I think its foundational element, the warm doughnut – which was topped with a big swirl of ice cream, drizzled with chocolate sauce and sprinkled with chopped roasted hazelnuts – reminded him of *loukoumades*, which are Greek syrupy doughnut balls. As a child, I was a Knickerbocker Glory girl. I think my parents thought of me as a health-conscious kid, ordering the dessert that would fulfil my five-a-day, as the fruit cocktail in it contained tinned peaches, pears, pineapple, grapes and cherries. But really, I just liked being able to order a dessert with the word 'knickers' in it.

The story of Serge's dating life was unlike the McDonald's slogan. Usually, by the time he got to the third date he wasn't 'lovin' it', so he would call things off. Once it was off, it was off: there was no going back and repeating with any of his dates. Serge said he preferred to 'move on'. He'd been talking about this today in our third session, prior to the (Freudian) slip about his twenty-year repeated lunch. Last week, Serge had matched with a woman on an online dating site. Their first date had been coffee. Their second date had been cocktails (followed by sex). Their third date, last night, had been dinner and a movie. Serge had sent the woman a text when he got home saying 'it wasn't working' for him. When I asked him what he meant by that, he said there was no 'vibe' or 'click' or 'spark'. This had been the case with every single woman he'd talked about in our sessions so far. Other than what they had eaten and whether they'd had sex, Serge never remembered a lot about his dates. He quickly forgot first names once it was over. Many of Serge's dates were one-night stands. Drive thrus, you might say. Just like his food, he quickly filled up, then it was finished and he didn't have to think about it.

Far be it for me to say who should fill up who and in what way. But people come to therapy because they want to change something about themselves and their lives. Serge wasn't living the life he wanted. He was serial dating when what he really wanted was a serious relationship and to settle down. He'd repeatedly said in our first session, 'I'm already thirty. I really wanna get married and have kids. When's it going to happen?' The big clue as to why this wasn't happening was in what Serge had just said about his lunch: he didn't want to 'think about it'. Serge wanted to 'drive thru' his thoughts and feelings, shutting them down in the same way he did his dates. These avoidant responses are what researchers refer to as deactivating attachment strategies. Serge didn't seem to be interested in exploring with me what was going on for him beneath the surface, psychologically or emotionally. In fact, his lack of interest bordered on boredom.

Serge yawned repeatedly during our session that day. I asked him why he was so tired. He said he'd gone to McDonald's on the way home from his date the night before, and by that time it was after midnight. I am all for a midnight Nigella-style fridge raid, but I found it interesting that Serge had gone to McDonald's after eating a substantial amount on his date, given that they'd had pick 'n' mix and popcorn and nachos at the cinema followed by a three-course dinner. And, of course, he'd had his chicken sandwich and crisps for lunch. So he'd eaten well that day. I pointed this out to Serge. He laughed a little nervously and said, 'I had to go. I fancied a McFlurry and you can't get them anywhere else.'

I grabbed the opportunity to pick up on the feeling of love that he had mentioned previously.

'Yes, I know; you said you "loved it" last session,' I said, wanting to show that I had held in mind what he'd said.

'Did I?' Serge looked surprised.

'Yes. I thought it was interesting when you said that. Sometimes we can love places, in the same way we love people,' I said. It's true: place attachment is a real thing. I once did some research on it, and attaching to places is just like attaching to people – it fulfils some of the same emotional and psychological needs. You can seek out a place for comfort and security in the same way you can seek out a person.

It turned out that McDonald's had a significant place in Serge's heart. He told me that as a child he would seek refuge there when his mother and father argued. He said that 'they were constantly at each other's throats'. Serge suspected his father was an alcoholic. Every night when his father came home from the pub, his parents would fight. Serge described hearing smashes and thuds from his bedroom. The morning after, he would sometimes see blood on the walls that looked like dried-up ketchup. Whenever things 'kicked off' at home, Serge would go to McDonald's. He said it was the only place where he 'felt okay', but it seemed like more than that. McDonald's was Serge's safe haven. It was open twenty-four hours a day, and available whenever he needed. There were no big surprises. Everything was as expected, from the cheery 'Hi, welcome to McDonald's!' greeting to the food itself. The burgers were consistent, from the Big Mac that had two all-beef patties, special sauce, lettuce, cheese, pickles and onions, to the McChicken Sandwich that contained crispy-coated chicken with lettuce and sandwich sauce. Serge's order was always the same: a McChicken Sandwich and fries, followed by a McFlurry.

When Serge was ten years old, something unexpected happened: his father left for another woman. Serge's half-brother was born six months later. Serge never saw his father very often after that. He didn't even really get to say a proper goodbye when it all happened. It was curious that Serge didn't remember much after his father left, but what he did remember was that his mother was never the same after that, and neither was their food life.

Serge said that his mother was a good cook when he was a child; there was always a homemade meal on the table and they stuck to a routine, which involved fish on a Friday and roast chicken on a Sunday. After his father left, Serge's mother became unwell with all sorts of ailments that doctors couldn't explain, which made me wonder if her symptoms were a psychosomatic response to the trauma of being abandoned by Serge's father. His mother stopped doing things at home, including cooking, and she didn't leave the house much. She would give Serge money to buy their food from the Peterl station at the end of the road. The only options there were processed, ready-made and frozen foods. Serge took over the 'cooking'. Now their food routine included things like fish fingers for dinner and something sweet and out of a packet that was quick and filling, like a flapjack or a doughnut, for breakfast (incidentally, all of those foods feature in *Cook, Eat, Repeat*). At the weekend, Serge's mother would give him money to buy himself a McDonald's. Serge would go on his own, and he would sit and eat a McChicken Sandwich and fries, followed by a McFlurry. Serge said his mother didn't eat much, and that 'she's basically lived on tea and toast since dad walked out'. Serge's mother had also stopped making his packed lunch for school after his father left. So every morning Serge started making himself a packed lunch. It was the same lunch he'd lived on ever since: a chicken sandwich and a packet of cheese and onion crisps.

Serge still lived at home with his mother. Over the years she had become more isolated and depressed, and she still didn't leave the house much. Serge said she basically read the television guide and watched television all day. As an adult, Serge had taken over the rent and the bills. He said they were able to manage on his salary as an accountant. Serge also paid for private health insurance so that his mother's medical issues could be taken care of quickly, and he accompanied her to all her appointments for her unexplained symptoms. As for the food shopping, Serge still did that too. While he now went to the supermarket and not the Peterl station for their shop, Serge said it was just 'quicker and easier' to keep it the same every week, and his mother liked it that way. It seemed that Serge had formed his life around taking care of his mother. He was pretty preoccupied with her. It was like he had turned into her surrogate husband.

This is probably the time to tell you that Serge's mother was called Andrea.

Freud would definitely have something to say about that.

Freud would also have said that Serge's repetitions were in some way bringing him back into the situation of his early trauma. As a result, part of what Serge was re-experiencing each time was unpleasure. It's what Freud called the compulsion to repeat, which he first wrote about in his paper *Remembering, Repeating and Working-Through*. Freud noticed that soldiers returning from World War Two would unconsciously repeat painful experiences in their dreams, instead of consciously remembering them. This is why he famously said that dreams are the royal road to the unconscious. But I disagree with Freud slightly because, as you can see from Serge, food is too.

Bowlby disagreed with Freud about a lot of things. Many years ago, I was asked to transcribe the last-ever interview Bowlby gave before he died in 1991, and at some points on the tape he got pretty heated about how much Freud emphasised inner stuff, things like dreams and fantasy and wishful thinking and forces of life and death. Bowlby was much more interested in outer stuff: real-life events, in other words. He was one of the first people to say that what happens to you matters for your mental health. Separations and losses matter, and Serge had experienced both.

Bowlby would have said that Serge's repetitions were attempts to meet his need for attachment security. But his strategy wasn't working. I understand there are times when we all might fancy a McFlurry, but it had got to the stage where Serge's repetitions had hijacked his ability to think, feel, remember, or do anything different. Why not go to Wimpy or why not have a different sandwich or why not date someone more than three times? This wasn't the comfort of the familiar; it was the safety of exactly the same. And it was keeping him safe from loss. After all, if Serge did get married and move on, he would lose his mother: she would no longer be his first and foremost attachment figure.

In our session that day, Serge had started remembering and we had started working through. I felt quite hopeful. As he left, I said I was looking forward to seeing him next week. Serge responded as he usually did: 'Sounds good.' After he was gone, I found myself thinking about something Freud said that I do agree with, which is quite lovely: 'How bold one gets when one is sure of being loved'. Maybe McDonald's didn't have to be Serge's only safe haven. If the therapy relationship could start to meet his needs for love and security then, slowly but surely, Serge might feel bold enough to not repeat.

***

The next week, the day before I was due to see Serge, an email popped up in my inbox.

> Hi Andrea,
>
> I don't think this is working for me. I've decided that I want to take a break from therapy so would like to stop our sessions.
>
> Thanks so much for all your help over the past few weeks.
>
> Kind regards,
> Serge

It was a break-up email.
It was also a repetition.

We had met three times, like his dates. It wasn't working out for him, like his dates. But there had been a spark, unlike on his dates; it just wasn't the sort of spark Serge wanted. His thoughts and feelings were starting to heat up. And so Serge was stopping therapy for the same reason I once spat out a McDonald's apple pie: it was too hot to handle. This repetition was precisely what we needed to work through in therapy, and we couldn't do that work if Serge called things off. I disagreed with stopping. I didn't want to fight with him, but I wanted to fight *for* him and show him that I thought our work was valuable and worth continuing. There was nothing to lose now by saying this. Rather than just waving Serge off as he moved on, I took a risk in my reply:

Hi Serge,

Thank you for your email and for sharing your thoughts.

I've been thinking a lot about our work, and I'm going to share what's going through my mind; it would be remiss of me not to right now. I'm sorry to hear that you would like to stop our sessions. But I do think your feelings about therapy not working for you are worth exploring, and could shed some light on the issues you came to see me for. We have an opportunity here and now to understand something valuable and I want to suggest that we take this and continue our sessions.

How does this sound to you?

With best wishes,
Andrea

I never heard from Serge again.

As Bowlby said, we do as we have been done by. Unsurprisingly, this is what Serge had done. His father had left him and now he had left me.

But Serge had also done something he had never done before: he had left Andrea. Sort of. I was the Andrea he could leave, unlike his mother.

Would Serge have thought about it — me, the therapy — after our email exchange? His twenty-year lunch mantra told me the likely answer to that was no. I did think about it though, a lot. I imagine my feelings were not so different from those of Serge's dates; I was sad and disappointed, and I repeatedly thought that I had done something wrong. I wasn't being over the top; I was just being human. A loss is a loss, whether it's my patient or anybody else. For me, goodbyes, especially the ones that don't feel so good, open up old wounds.

However, I was emotionally efficient in the sense that I sought help from my Delia. Together we worked through the feelings of loss that were being repeated in me as a result.

I also sought out Nigella Lawson. Not literally, but remember I said that food writing has a lot to say about attachment and love? Nigella says that cook, eat, repeat is more than just a mantra; it's the story of her life. And in *Cook, Eat, Repeat*, I found a whole list on why this is, and what food is for her. It helped me to understand what food – and life – sadly wasn't for Serge: it wasn't a constant pleasure, he didn't think greedily about it, he didn't reflect deeply on it, he didn't learn from it and it didn't provide comfort, inspiration, meaning or beauty.

Cooking, eating chicken sandwiches (both his own and at McDonald's) and repeating would be the story of Serge's life, it seemed.

But it would be in a very non-Nigella way.

* * *

Cheese and Onion Crisp-Chips

This is my homage to the other part of Serge's lunch, with inspiration from Nigella Lawson and her recipe for salt and vinegar potatoes, which made me see how classic crisp flavours punch above their weight in hot potato form.

Serves 2

500g smallish potatoes
1 teaspoon salt
4 tablespoons vegetable oil
4 tablespoons grated Parmesan
3 tablespoons onion granules
Sea salt flakes, to finish

Preheat the oven to 220°C/200°C fan/gas mark 7.

Peel the potatoes, cut them into slices around 5mm thick, then place in a large saucepan with just enough cold water to cover them, along with ½ teaspoon salt. Bring to the boil, lower the heat and cover the pan. Gently boil the potatoes for about 5 minutes.

Drain the potatoes well and leave them in a colander over the pan to steam-dry for a few minutes.

Pour the vegetable oil into a large roasting tin and pop it in the oven for around 5 minutes. While the oil is heating, prepare the seasoning by combining the grated Parmesan, onion granules and remaining ½ teaspoon of salt. Use a fork to mix in a small bowl, or put the whole lot into a jar and shake vigorously.

Take the roasting tin out of the oven and add the potato slices to the hot oil. As the slices come into contact with the fat they will sizzle sharply, so take care. Turn the potato slices in the oil, making sure they are evenly coated. Ensure you have given the slices as much space as possible; they shouldn't be overcrowded, as they will steam instead of roast and you won't get crispy edges. Return the tin to the oven and roast for 20 minutes, then turn the slices over and roast for another 10 minutes.

Now to cheese and onion-ify the potatoes: take the tin out of the oven and sprinkle the slices with the seasoning. Pop them back in the oven for around 5 minutes. The purpose of this final blast of heat is only for the seasoning to stick to the spuds; you don't want them to become too bronzed.

Remove from the oven and sprinkle the cheese and onion crisp-chips with sea salt flakes. Serve as a side to grilled chicken or steak, or simply eat them on their own.

13

Procrastibaking

If you put off painful feelings, where else might you find them?

I have learned a lot about food, love and loss from my patients, but also from the students I teach at university. There is one student in particular who comes to mind. Her name was Sophia, and she was studying for a Master's in Psychological Therapies and Interventions. I would see Sophia every week for the module I taught on psychotherapy. She was charming, and made valuable contributions in each session. However, these contributions took on a different form during the second semester, when she started to bring in baked goods for her classmates. Sophia's offerings made class feel like *The Great British Bake-Off*, and each week was themed, just like the show: first came cakes (mini Victoria sponges), followed by biscuits (Viennese whirls), then we had bread (iced buns), patisserie was after that (choux buns), and then, of course, there was chocolate (brownies). There was even a 'German week' when she made a German chocolate pie, which, it turns out, isn't even German: it's a sweet pastry case filled with rich fudgy chocolate, desiccated coconut and chopped pecans. It was named after a man whose name was German, not a man from Germany.

I noticed that all of this baking was happening during the time when Sophia and her classmates had several course-work deadlines. Sophia had already missed three of these; if she missed any more, she was in danger of failing the module, and quite possibly her whole Master's degree. At the end of class one day, as her peers were digging into the German chocolate pie, I asked Sophia if we could have a chat afterwards in the privacy of my office. In our meeting, I expressed my concerns and asked her if anything was the matter. Sophia told me she was scared of 'not doing well'. The feeling had become so overwhelming that she would freeze whenever she attempted to do any of her assignments.

'I can't think. I can't read. I sit at the computer, my mind goes blank and I can't write. I just get so scared I'm going to fail. To my parents, anything less than a Distinction isn't good enough. In their eyes, it means I've failed,' she said, looking tearful. I could see there was a lot at stake for Sophia. Now her baking made sense: at least that was good enough, and she hadn't failed her friends.

The paradox was that Sophia's fear of failure was putting her at risk of actual failure. I told Sophia I understood the pressure she was under, but perhaps we could think together about what would be possible for her.

'What is it you feel you *can* do?' I asked.

Her reply wasn't exactly what I was expecting.

'Bake,' she said instantly. 'I'm baking to avoid doing my coursework. Well, to avoid feeling the feelings about my coursework. I'm procrastibaking.'

So, Sophia was procrastinating by baking. I could think of worse ways to put off feelings. As she told me, I found myself smiling for two reasons. First, I was delighted to see that Sophia had a sound understanding of the defence known as displacement, and how it was playing out in her own life. Second, I could empathise. I too was once a pro-crastibaker. A long time ago.

***

It's Saturday 17 July 1993, and my mother is standing in the kitchen and she is cooking. Actually, she is moving around the kitchen quite a lot. My mother is making a Greek dish called *macaronia tou fournou*, which means 'macaroni of the oven'. It is the Cypriot version of what you might know from a Greek island holiday as the more poetical *pastitsio*. It's a layered and baked pasta, a bit like a lasagne. So far, my mother has completed two parts of the recipe: she has boiled the pasta, the *macaronia*, and she has made the meat sauce, which is similar to a Bolognese. Both the *macaronia* and the meat sauce have been layered inside a rectangular dish, which sits on the counter waiting patiently.

I am watching and helping my mother cook. Although at the moment, I am not helping: I am standing at the counter stealing the long, squiggly *macaronia* from the dish and dipping them into the mound of grated halloumi speckled with dried mint that my mother prepped earlier. My mother smiles at me with her eyes; she knows this is my favourite bit. I am ten years old, impatient and not interested in delaying gratification until the finished dish. As far as I'm concerned, I am eating the most delicious thing in the world: the pasta has a chicken stock cube savouriness leftover from its boiling liquid, the halloumi gives it an ever-so-slight saltiness and the dried mint is a tiny bit sweet. Together, it is perfect.

My mother is now making the white sauce. She breaks three eggs into a bowl and beats them with a fork. Her hand is clenched around the fork to form a fist and her wrist action is swift, as if she is doing rounds on a punchball. The eggs have frothed so much they look like one of those foamy cappuccinos my mother loves. She leaves the eggs aside, strides to the fridge and takes out the margarine. She scoops it straight from the tub into a saucepan, puts the pan on the cooker and turns on the heat. As the margarine melts in the saucepan, my mother adds flour and stirs to create soft golden lumps. She starts to trickle in the milk. The baby lumps drink it up, thirstily. Little by little, my mother pours in the rest of the milk and switches to her balloon whisk. It doesn't take long for the lumps to disappear. They won't come back now. She takes the saucepan off the stove and gradually whisks the beaten eggs into the sauce. The pan goes back on the heat. My mother's whisking slows down as the sauce starts to thicken. Now we just have to wait for the sign that it's ready.

The phone rings.

'Andrea, keep an eye on the sauce for me. You know what to look for? When it goes "poof poof", switch off the gas,' my mother says as she walks towards the phone, which is mounted on the wall by the kitchen door. She is referring to when the thickened sauce starts to make craters that 'poof' on the surface. Then you know it's done. I skip a short distance along the counter until I reach the cooker. Then I stop and stand, and watch.

A minute later, my mother is no longer standing. She has dropped the phone and is clutching the wall. The handset bounces up and down, like someone on a bungee cord. The phone does a dizzy twirl, then it just dangles, which is what my mother is doing now. My father's attention has been taken away from the television in the living room and he has rushed to my mother. He is bent over, trying to hoist her back onto her feet, but she is like a floppy baby who can't hold herself up. My father, whom I have always considered to be a strong man, is struggling. My mother has become a dead weight. But her voice is alive. I'm not allowed to watch horror movies, but if I were, this is what I imagine the screaming would sound like. Monster screams. She is screaming one thing, over and over: 'I didn't get to say goodbye'. At that moment, all the pain in the world is in our kitchen, and in my mother's body. The screaming turns into sobbing. The tight curls of her perm are giving in and undoing themselves as her head hangs down. Tears fall out of her curls; it's like her hair is crying.

My father manages to get my mother to the kitchen table where we eat dinner every night. He puts her down onto a chair. My mother isn't sitting up. She slumps over the table, and her head twists to the side, facing me. Teardrops are still coming out of her eyes, but it's like someone has switched the light off inside them, as if no one is home.

I am standing in the kitchen, watching this person who is meant to be my mother.

I don't know what has happened, or who she hasn't said goodbye to.

I also don't know how my mother is ever going to stand up again.

I can smell burning. Oh no, the sauce. But it's too late. My teacher at school says you shouldn't cry over spilled milk. What about burned milk?

Soon, we are all crying.

There will be no *macaronia tou fournou* for dinner this Saturday night.

Or for the next ten years.

***

Macaroni comes from the Greek word *macaritis*, which means 'blessed'. In ancient Greek times, in order to be truly blessed you had to be dead. At funerals, grains were served to pay tribute to the dead person, as they journeyed to the world of the gods. Once there, they would no longer be burdened with earthly worries of pain and separation and loss – all of which came with the phone call on that

Saturday. The call was from a doctor in New Zealand, who had told my mother that her younger brother, George, who was thirty-two years old at the time, had died. They had switched off his life support machine and my beloved Uncle George had become a *macaritis* while my mother was cooking what happened to be his favourite dish.

Macaronia tou fournou was my uncle George's most-loved food. But one of the people he loved most, his mother (my grandmother) hadn't made it for him for many years. She was not a Pasta Granny, like the popular YouTube cooks. My maternal grandmother was a pissed-off granny. Just after Uncle George was out of his teenage years, she had what was then known as a nervous breakdown and left my grandfather. She moved to a small council flat in north London and hardly saw anyone after that. Her estrangement was from the kitchen, as well as the family. She stopped cooking. I guess she threw the generational gender rulebook out the window when she walked out on my grandfather. My grandmother chained-smoked, ate ready-made meals and watched Western movies; she worshipped Rock Hudson. Her version of Old West fare — in other words, beans, beef and taters — was Heinz baked beans, frozen Birds Eye burgers and Smash instant mashed potato.

I had never eaten my grandmother's *macaronia tou fournou*, but I ate my mother's often — she made it most Saturdays. There was also one day, about a year before that fateful Saturday in July, when she cooked the dish on a Wednesday. My uncle George was coming over for dinner on his way to the airport. He was leaving London and moving to New Zealand because he'd got a new job. He was going to start a new life.

I was happy for him, and at the same time, so sad for me. Uncle George was like my second father. I loved everything about him, even his thick, chevron moustache that would tickle when he kissed my forehead; those soft bristles always swept my pain away. He was absolutely one of my attachment figures. I started to miss Uncle George even before he left. I'd noticed that in the last few months he hadn't been to our house much at all, and certainly not for dinner. I suggested to my mother that it would be nice to have *macaronia tou fournou* as a going-away dinner for Uncle George, because it was his favourite and it would show him that we loved him. I wouldn't know until years later that I had Julia Child's confirmation: 'I think careful cooking is love, don't you?' she once said. I definitely did. My mother seemed to think so too, or at least she liked my idea. And so, dinner was planned for my uncle George's last night in London. My mother bought partyware because she said it was a special occasion: red plastic knives, forks and spoons and red paper plates with balloon borders and calligraphy writing in the middle that said 'Let's Celebrate!' I thought this was really weird. If it really was such a celebration, I wondered why we weren't using my mother's Royal Doulton chinaware, like we always did for special occasions. Anyway, at dinner on that Wednesday evening, I tried to do as the plate told me to, to be celebratory, with an exclamation mark. But I just couldn't. We tried to be normal even though there was clearly an elephant in the room, sitting at the table with us. I did my best to keep the conversation going by talking about my favourite topic: food. In an attempt to show how worldly I was for a ten-year-old, I said to Uncle George, 'They have famous lamb in New Zealand, don't they? You can make nice kleftiko!' He gazed lovingly at me.

As usual, I practically licked my plate clean. But my uncle George didn't. He looked anxious, so I wasn't surprised his appetite was affected. I've never liked food waste, even as a child, so I went to help myself to his leftovers. At that moment, my mother turned into The Flash: she whipped the plate away and put it straight in the bin. It was one of the strangest things I had ever seen her do.

Then it was time for Uncle George to go. I pulled over the nearest chair, stood on it and put my arms around his neck. It was like we were at a school disco with soft lights dancing around us, and he was the boy I loved most in the whole world. Because he was. As I looked at his face, into his eyes, I so wanted to say something 'wow' that he would remember forever. But I couldn't think of anything. I felt like I was running out of words. We were also running out of time. My heart pumped hotly in my little chest, like I was getting ready to jump off a cliff. So I just told the truth.

'I don't want you to go,' I said.

'I know,' he said. That was his response. Two whispered words. It was the most loving and understanding response I could wish for. My uncle George didn't try to convince me or contradict me or change my mind. He looked at me, into my eyes, and showed that he knew what was on my mind and in my heart. He took my feelings seriously. He got it.

I, however, didn't get it, because I hadn't been told the whole truth. We were separating and there would be no reunion. My uncle George was dying. I didn't know that would be the last time I would ever see him.

It was also the first time he didn't kiss me goodbye on my forehead, like he usually did.

***

On the afternoon of that Saturday my uncle George died, we broke the news to my grandparents. I had only ever known them separated and the situation between them wasn't a good one, so it felt strangely as though George wasn't 'their' son. While my mother stayed at home with my brother, and made a call to my grandmother to tell her that her son had died, my father and I drove to my grandfather's house to tell him that his son had died. When we arrived, my grandfather was in the living room watching television. I left my father there with him and went next door to the kitchen. I could hear them talking as I snooped around my grandfather's kitchen. We didn't see him often either, so I didn't know him that well. I looked in the cupboards and in the fridge for clues that would help me to understand my grandfather better, as a person, but I didn't find much more than mustard, cheese and bread. Understanding his marriage to my grandmother, however, was much easier. The writing was on the wall – literally. My grandmother had graffitied the kitchen before she walked out on him. There were a lot of F-words on those walls. She was pissed off even before she became my granny.

As I roamed around the kitchen, I could hear my father's and grandfather's conversation next door. My father was talking about what needed to be done, in terms of repatriating Uncle George's body from New Zealand and the funeral arrangements. After that, there was silence. Then my grandfather said, 'This is all so embarrassing.' His words stopped me cold. Then they upset me, even more than I already was. How could he say that? Although I didn't know much about grief, and this was my first experience of loss, I already knew that embarrassment wasn't part of it. I was devastated, and I couldn't understand why that wasn't my grandfather's first feeling in response to his son dying. My father and I left shortly after that, and I pretended that I hadn't heard what my grandfather had said.

In the car on the way home, my father and I had what I now call a 'shoulder to shoulder' conversation. If you're side by side with someone, like when you're in the car or walking, 'big' conversation topics tend to come up more easily because you're not under the gaze of the other person. If you don't see their eyes, you don't have to deal with their emotions and expectations. In the car that day, my father talked to me about some very big things, like life and death and destiny, and how his destiny had been to come to the UK when really he was meant to have gone to Australia (that was the first of his visa problems). When my father arrived in the 1970s, he got into the English punk music scene and, courtesy of the Sex Pistols, adopted his mantra for life, which he said to me while driving that Saturday afternoon: 'Andrea, with some people you have to never mind the bollocks.' I had no idea what my father meant by this and, of course, it wasn't exactly appropriate for a child. But let's face it, none of this was. But then we did do something appropriate for a child: we went to McDonald's and he bought me a Happy Meal. Earlier, after my mother had managed to stand up, she said we should all change into black clothing to show we were in mourning. In McDonald's, under the Golden Arches and against the cheerful, bright red and yellow, my father and I looked like the Addams Family. My father wasn't fond of McDonald's, so he didn't order anything for himself. After we got my meal, we went and sat on high stools at the counter by the window.

My father and I were side by side again.

It was time for another one of those conversations.

'You know your uncle George was a gay, don't you?' said my father, as I unwrapped my hamburger. I turned my attention away from the burger in my hands and looked up at my father. My head cocked to the side and I squinted at him, not because I didn't believe what he was saying, but because I was surprised by his use of the indefinite article. English was my best subject at school and to my knowledge, this was inappropriate noun usage. My father's grammar wasn't personal, it was a sign of the times. Then again, my father could have been telling me that Uncle George was a vegetarian or a trainspotter and I would have had the same (non)response. It made no difference to how I felt about my uncle, and how he felt about me. Love was love.

It was over that Happy Meal that I started to ask myself questions about love and relationships. Big questions. As all these questions went round and round in my mind, I began to eat my burger in big mouthfuls. If my mouth was full, I didn't risk the biggest question falling out of it, a question that had been stirring up since my grandfather's comment: your parents are meant to love you and be there for you no matter what, right? My family's story behind that, I would discover later, was a very unhappy one: my uncle George had felt such shame about being gay and having HIV that when the disease progressed he had gone to the other side of the world to die. He lived his last days lonely and isolated in a hospice in Auckland, where he died of AIDS-related complications. He was alone. He died without a hand to hold.

There was only one answer to my question: this wasn't love.

It was bollocks.

***

After Uncle George died, *macaronia tou fournou* became the traumatic and evil equivalent of the Proustian madeleine moment for my mother. She stopped making it, on Saturdays and every other day of the week. Saturday night became takeaway night. I noticed my mother never ate much, even when she had her beloved Big Mac for dinner. My mother became what attachment theory would call 'inaccessible': she was physically present but emotionally absent, except for her grief. Her tears left tracks on her face and all her hurt settled into them. My beautiful mother developed wrinkles that not even she could iron out.

Meanwhile, I was like a little emotional hoover, sucking up all of the unfelt feeling in the house, and there was no one to help me with it. Feelings have never been my father's forte.

I felt like a motherless child.

So I began procrastibaking. Now, I can see there were two reasons why. One, I was trying to avoid feeling my grief, because there was no one to feel it with. Two, it was part of my plan to find someone else – another mother – to attach to.

That someone else was Mrs Brady, my school teacher. She was American and actually looked a bit like Carol Brady of *The Brady Bunch*, but her first name was Anne. I wanted nothing more than to be her favourite pupil. I loved her because she was warm and caring and she didn't ever poo-poo anybody's contributions in class. She wore chunky jewellery that looked like supersized M&Ms. I was fascinated by her soft, ever so slightly nasal accent. Because of Mrs Brady, I became interested in all foodie things Americana. What were these sweet foreign treats called Tootsie Rolls and Twinkies? Cupcakes, on the other hand, I understood, because they were pretty much fairy cakes. I decided that the way to Mrs Brady's heart was through her stomach via little cakes with icing, topped with silver balls, jelly diamonds, hundreds and thousands and anything else I could think of. In my mind the recipe was simple: if I baked fairy cakes for Mrs Brady, she would love me and we would have a special bond. That was the attachment plan. The practical plan was to make them at the weekend with the intention of taking them in for Mrs Brady and saying 'Ta-da!' on Monday morning, and for that part I was armed and ready with my *Ladybird Book of Making and Decorating Cakes*.

You know the recipe: it's the one from Chapter 5.

The problem was that for some reason the recipe didn't work. Or I couldn't bake. Or both. Try as I might, again and again, weekend after weekend, my cakes came out wrong. They looked nothing like the picture in my book, in which a little girl was smiling proudly at a doily-covered plate of perfectly risen fairy cakes. I would later learn that the technical term for my cakes was (ironically) 'sad', which is what I was too every Saturday when I looked at my sunken cakes. My book had a 'What Went Wrong' section at the back, which I would read obsessively. I took on board the suggestions, which included trying another method, using different brands of ingredients and not overbeating the mixture (I am my mother's daughter, so heavy-handed whisking comes with the territory). None of it made any difference. Whenever the kitchen timer went off and I opened the oven door, my hope would plummet as much as my cakes. Another batch of cakes for the bin. Another week when I wouldn't be able to show my love for Mrs Brady in baked form. Saturdays became Bake, Don't Eat, Repeat.

Eventually, after months of failed fairy cakes, I made some that were good enough to give to Mrs Brady. I asked my mother if she had a paper plate that I could put them on to take them into school. She did have paper plates: the leftover 'Let's Celebrate!' ones she had used for my uncle George's last *macaronia tou fournou* supper. They had been in the cupboard ever since. I later found out why we had used partyware on the day that had been anything but a party: apparently some quack doctor, who was a family friend, told my mother that it was best if Uncle George had his own crockery and cutlery (and toilet seat) at the advanced stage of the illness. More bollocks.

As a family, we didn't talk about sexually transmitted infections, or sex or sexuality very well. Neither did attachment theory. At the time, Ainsworth, more than Bowlby, talked about the importance of sex, attachment and caregiving in adult romantic relationships. And it's still only very recently that attachment research has become more inclusive of diversity in sexual orientation. My ten-year-old self would be comforted to know that all of these different studies are coming to the same conclusion as she did that day sitting in McDonald's eating her Happy Meal: love is love.

***

For my mother, *macaronia tou fournou* remained repressed for a long time. It was her version of procrastibaking. She put off making it for over ten years, and with it all the feelings associated with losing her little brother. She also put off telling me the real story about Uncle George; it was just too painful for her, and she was also trying to protect me. She did what she thought was best. We inevitably ended up in the same boat: I didn't get to say goodbye to him either, which was another loss. Children always need to be kept in the know when someone is dying. They might need the knowledge in child-friendly terms, but they need the truth from their attachment figures. Otherwise, the secure base becomes insecure. When trust is broken like that, it can take years to rebuild. It did for me and my mother.

When I moved into my first flat in my twenties, I asked my mother if she would help me cook for a dinner party I was having one evening. She agreed. And it was there, in the shoebox kitchen of my newly rented flat, while my mother and I stood shoulder to shoulder making *macaronia tou fournou*, that we started to say what had gone unsaid for a long, long time.

* * *

Macaronia tou Fournou

My mother's recipe, in its original and blessed form. *Macaronia* are a thick, spaghetti-like pasta with holes through the middle. I've always thought that *macaronia* look as though they belong in a church, and the idea of a long, thin candle of pasta feels fitting for this story.

Serves 8

For the *macaronia*:
1 chicken stock cube
500g *macaronia* (Greek brands will call it size 1 or 2 Pastitsio pasta. Bucatini pasta would work well too)

For the meat sauce:
3 tablespoons olive oil
1 medium onion, peeled and finely chopped
500g minced pork (or you could use half pork and half beef)
10g flat-leaf parsley, finely chopped
1 teaspoon dried mint
1 teaspoon salt
½ teaspoon ground black pepper
⅛ teaspoon ground cinnamon
1 x 227g tin plum tomatoes, crushed (use your hands or a fork)

To assemble:
200g halloumi, grated
½ teaspoon dried mint

For the white sauce:
3 large eggs
60g margarine or butter
60g plain flour
⅛ teaspoon salt
500ml full-fat or semi-skimmed milk
¼ teaspoon freshly grated nutmeg

Grease a rectangular ovenproof dish (approximately 32 x 23 x 6cm deep) with a little oil and preheat the oven to 200°C/180°C fan/gas mark 6.

Bring a large pan of water to the boil, dissolve the chicken stock cube in it, then add the pasta. Cook according to the instructions on the packet, or until al dente. Drain the pasta in a colander, then run cold water over the *macaronia* for about 30 seconds to prevent them from sticking together. Leave aside in the colander to continue cooling and draining.

To make the meat sauce, heat the olive oil in a large saucepan over medium heat. Add the onion and cook for a few minutes, until the pieces are a pale golden colour and softened.

Crumble in the minced meat, turn up the heat to medium-high and fry the meat until browned. Stir the mince continuously to stop it forming lumps (use a fork if necessary to break it up).

Add the flat-leaf parsley, dried mint, salt, pepper and cinnamon to the browned mince. Add the crushed tomatoes. Bring to the boil, turn down the heat and let the sauce cook for 10 minutes. Remove from the heat and set aside.

In the meantime, start assembling the *macaronia tou fournou*. Mix the grated halloumi with the dried mint. Put half the pasta into the dish and spread it out evenly. Add the meat sauce on top, making sure to cover all of the pasta. Sprinkle one quarter of the grated halloumi mixture over the meat. Put the other half of the pasta on top, again spreading it out evenly.

To make the white sauce, first beat the eggs, then set aside. Melt the margarine/butter in a medium saucepan over a gentle heat. Add the flour and salt and keep stirring with a wooden spoon to form a paste (this is the roux). Cook the roux for a couple of minutes, until it is smooth, soft and golden.

Turn up the heat to medium. Add a quarter of the milk and stir until it is combined into the roux. Add another quarter of the milk and stir it into the roux. Pour in the rest of the milk and stir continuously; it's best to use a whisk now. Keep whisking until you can see no lumps. Remove the pan from the heat and gradually whisk in the beaten eggs. Once the eggs are incorporated, return the pan to a gentle heat and keep whisking until you have a thick, smooth sauce. In 1–2 minutes you will see small craters start to form on the surface (what my mother calls 'poof poof'). This tells you the sauce is ready. Stir in the remaining grated halloumi mixture and the grated nutmeg.

Pour the white sauce into the dish, making sure to cover all of the pasta. Bake the *macaronia tou fournou* for approximately 45 minutes. When it's ready, the top will look like a patchwork quilt of honey gold, golden brown and slightly scorched spots (these are nothing to worry about, it's where the higher concentrations of halloumi are in the sauce). Leave to cool slightly before cutting and serving. You can eat this at room temperature too; that's how my uncle George liked it best.

14

Grief, Eggs and Ham

Would you, could you, let your love live
on after loss?

I have never had a patient cook attachment theory, until
I met Calvin. And I do mean 'cook' quite literally.

Before I tell you about Calvin, I want to tell you about
another man, named Colin Murray Parkes, who was a
collaborator of Bowlby's. Parkes thought the best way to
answer the question of 'What is love?' was by working with
those who had lost love. He and Bowlby were the first to
research bereavement in adults, and their findings have been
so important for showing how humans move through grief.

Years ago, Parkes invited me and two of my psychotherapist colleagues to spend the day with him at his home.
I was going to meet an attachment theory celebrity – how
exciting! In real life, Parkes felt like Hertfordshire's very
own BFG: he was tall and gangly in a gentle way, with that
special grandpa growth of wild white hair and bright eyes.
He was friendly, as well as benevolent and generous. We
spent all day talking about death, dying, grief, mourning
and the most painful forms of loss, but Parkes spoke about

it all in the spirit of love. He was even more sunny-side-up than the eggs we had for lunch at the pub. He told me, over ham, egg and chips, something I will never forget: that grief and love are two sides of the same coin.

Eggs are relevant to the story I am about to tell you, and my lunch on that memorable day with Parkes is not the only reason why.

***

I met Calvin a few months after his father died. He was in his late thirties, married with a young son. I found him very warm at our first meeting, and he seemed eager to engage in therapy to help him with his grief. Calvin's father had died after a long struggle with cancer. The disease, however, didn't affect their bond, which remained secure and loving right until the end. In preparation for his father's death, Calvin had read up on palliative care, and when his father lost his appetite, Calvin knew it was nearly time. It's true: food is part of our first relationship and our first hello to our attachment figure, and it's also our first goodbye to the world. At his bedside, Calvin told his father he would continue their 'thing': every Saturday morning they would go to the caff for a full English breakfast. The unique thing about their 'thing' was the sauce they had: not red or brown, but white: salad cream made Calvin his 'father's son'. I said to Calvin that must have been difficult, to think about their thing – the caff, the breakfast – without his father.

'Yeah, but it was harder to think he was hanging on for me. Even harder than watching him go through chemo, and that was hard: they were killing the tumour but it felt like they were killing him in the process. He'd been dying for a long time. By saying that about the caff, it was like I was telling him, "Hey, it's okay, Dad, you can go, you don't need to hang on here for me. I'll be all right",' said Calvin. I remember in one of my own therapy sessions, Delia quoted Samuel Beckett: 'Death is dead and no more dying'. For Calvin, his father's dying had hurt more than his death, and Calvin's promise to continue their food ritual had been part of giving his father permission to die.

Calvin's grief had a different flavour to that I'd seen in other patients. I remember Parkes saying that when people write books about the psychology of sex, they aren't pornographic, so similarly, when it comes to grief, people needn't be doleful. And Calvin wasn't a lot of the time, both in our sessions as well as outside. About the burial, Calvin said, 'I wanted to celebrate my dad's life and put the "fun" in funeral' – and that's exactly what he did. Calvin gave himself the go-ahead to feel his feelings and to find things out. He fed his curiosity by immersing himself in any and all literature on grief, from Dylan Thomas to Charles Darwin. Speaking of whom, I could see what Darwin called 'grief muscles' on Calvin's face: the furrows formed just on the middle part of his forehead. They also showed when he asked me questions, which he did a lot at the start of his therapy.

'What is grief?' Calvin asked in one of our earliest sessions.

'Grief is the reaction to losing something we love – a person or even an object. The intense pining, that's what we call separation anxiety. Grieving adults have the same response as children who are separated from their parents,' I said.

'How is that different from bereavement?' said Calvin.

'Bereavement is much more than just grief. It's about the major changes we go through after a loss. Sometimes bereavement is associated with things like memory flash-backs or feelings of blame or shame or guilt. These aren't part of grief, but they might complicate grief,' I said.

'Is more than just grief what they call "complicated grief", then?' he asked.

'Yes. In a way, you could say it's more grief,' I said. 'Complicated grief is when grief goes on for an unusually long time and gets in the way of usual, daily life. It's complicated because it can lead to mental health problems, like depression.'

'What is "grief work"?' asked Calvin.

'That's what you and I are doing right now,' I said.

Calvin asked me so many questions that, on the surface, it seemed as though our initial sessions were Q&As. But I sensed there was something deeper to Calvin's questioning. This was his first experience of therapy and he had come having lost his father, one of his attachment figures. Calvin had just met me; I was effectively a stranger to him.

I wondered if his real question was about our relationship. If Calvin could trust my answers, perhaps he could trust me. That was going to be the most important – and complicated – part of our work in therapy.

Calvin was bookish, but he wasn't a textbook patient. As time went on, I witnessed him going through what Parkes and Bowlby called the 'phases of grief', but not in sequence; Calvin oscillated back and forth between the three phases of: numbing (he felt stunned and unable to accept the news that his father was really gone); yearning and searching for the lost loved one (he had pangs of intense pining for his father); and despair and disorganisation (he felt hopeless about whether he would be able to salvage himself). I've always thought the phases of grief almost sound like the steps of a recipe, but Parkes said the intention was never for the concept to be used in that way; the point was to recognise that grief is a process, and not necessarily a simple one. It wasn't until the 1990s when research started to show that a lot of patients fitted the model, but the fourth phase, reorganisation, was where they stumbled; their lives had moved on but the pain remained. What these people were doing, and what this has become known as, is growing around grief.

It has also since been called the fried egg model of grief.

A little while into our work, I found myself mentioning this to Calvin. I told him I'd been holding him in mind and that I'd thought of something he might find helpful. The thing is, it's not often that a scientific or psychological theory references fried eggs, so when I said 'fried egg model of grief', Calvin looked at me like I had egg on my face. The only way to clear up his confusion was to show him, not tell him, so I grabbed my notepad and a pencil from the desk behind me. I turned to a fresh sheet of paper and drew a circle.

'Calvin, imagine this circle represents you,' I said. Then I drew another circle inside, nearly as big as the first, and I shaded it in, 'This shaded circle represents your grief. See how it takes up so much room? That's because at first the grief is so self-consuming,' I said.

Calvin nodded and I noticed that his forehead looked less crinkled and confused. Satisfied that he had digested this drawing, I rolled up my sleeves and got ready for the next one. This time, I sketched the grief circle first and shaded it in. Then I drew a much bigger circle around it. I looked at Calvin, as I continued my explanation. 'But as the days, months and years pass, this outer circle grows bigger as you have new experiences beyond your grief. So, even though the grief is still there, it will take up a smaller part of you and your life.' Finally, I said: 'Can you see how it looks like a fried egg? The white is your whole self and the yolk is your grief.'

As we ended that day's session, I found myself wanting to give Calvin something to take away. I tore the page with my drawings out of my notepad and handed it to him. Winnicott would have called this a transitional object: an object that goes on being important. I didn't realise at the time just how transitional it would be for Calvin.

The next week, Calvin came in and said to me: 'Andrea, I cooked the theory.'

What on earth he was talking about? I hadn't heard anything like this before – here, there or anywhere in attachment theory, research or therapy.

Calvin's face looked serious, whereas mine was seriously confused. The feeling on my face also came out in my response to him: I simply said, 'Huh?'

Then it was Calvin's turn to explain.

'On Saturday, I tried to go to the caff, but I couldn't bring myself to go. I just had this pang of grief that paralysed me,' he said. 'I sat there in the kitchen, all morning. I thought about what you said, or drew, for me last session. And then I decided to cook it. I cooked a fried egg. Or, really, egg in a hole.'

For Calvin, the method was more psychological than gastronomical. He explained: 'I cut out the bread with a really small cup so that when I cracked the egg in, the white didn't spread out at all, because of the big bread barrier. That day, my grief felt like it took up pretty much all of me. It was sort of symbolic to see it there in front of me.'

'It's certainly creative. But it sounds like it was cathartic too, a way of releasing something,' I said.

'Yeah, it was. I did have a little cry. Sam came into the kitchen and noticed I was sad. I said I was sad because I miss grandpa. He gave me a hug; it was really sweet. I read that you're supposed to tell kids the truth when a person dies and not just say they've gone to heaven. Sam's only eight, but I've been honest about telling him that grandpa has died which means we won't see him again, and it's okay for us to be upset,' Calvin said. I was struck by his tenderness and thoughtfulness. And I couldn't help but feel sad about the hole in my own parallel experience, when my uncle George died. I continued to listen, as Calvin shared more about the conversation with his son.

'I explained to Sam that my egg in a hole showed how I was feeling. The white was the whole of me, and the yolk was the part that misses Grandpa. And he totally got it. He said, 'Daddy, all of you misses Grandpa.' And I said yes, I do right now. Then Sam asked if we could make an egg in the hole for him too. He chose a much bigger cup to cut out the hole with, so there was more egg white in his one. I told Sam that as time goes by, that's what my egg in a hole will look like. Even though the yolk will still be there and I'll still miss Grandpa, it won't take up all of me like it does now — the white bit of me will get bigger as we go to great places together and more fun things start to happen,' said Calvin.

And that was how eggs became relevant to Calvin's personal experience of grief. He literally modelled his grief by making egg in a hole. If I ever wanted an answer to the question of whether Calvin trusted me, here it was — and it wasn't complicated. He had taken what I had given him and he had run with it. Or, he had cooked it. Every week, Calvin would cook egg in a hole according to how he felt. And every week he would tell me about it in our session, and together we talked about his feelings and the meaning it held for him. Initially, Calvin's bread-hole-cutting utensils were espresso cups and cookie cutters. Over time, he began to use saucers and bowls. The whites in Calvin's eggs in holes grew when he felt able to grow other parts of his life. Sam was, of course, a big part of this. Eventually, Calvin visited the caff that he and his father used to go to every Saturday, and before long he started to take Sam with him, which they both loved and looked forward to (although Sam preferred a bacon butty with tomato ketchup to a full English soused in salad cream).

The fried egg model of grief tells us that the pain doesn't go away after someone dies. But the love doesn't go away either. Would you, could you, let the love be? Yes, you can. In *Loss*, Bowlby said something I think any person grieving would find comforting: that you can keep a lost loved one as a secure attachment figure. In fact, if you let these feelings of attachment continue, you will be able to reorganise your life in a way that is so much more meaningful. Or, in Calvin's case, sunny side up.

* * *

Egg in a Hole

For modelling grief. Or just for breakfast.

Serves 1

1 egg
1 slice of bread

2 tablespoons olive oil or butter
Sea salt flakes, to finish

Cut out a hole in the bread with whatever utensil you like.

Heat the olive oil or butter in a small frying pan over medium-high heat. Fry the bread for a couple of minutes, then flip it over.

Crack the egg into the hole. Turn the heat down to avoid the bread burning and cook for 5 minutes, or until the egg is set. Season with sea salt flakes and serve.

15

What We Talk About When We Talk About Cake

Do you ever get over someone you've lost?

A year after Bruno and I broke up, I found myself in an area of London that we used to visit together often, mostly because it had a Byron Burgers. There was also an independent record shop there that Bruno loved. No, scratch that. He adored it, or to be more accurate, he adored the people who worked there. I suspect there was some attachment yearning to it because the folk running the shop were very nurturing of new artists and bands. Did I mention that Bruno was a musician? It wasn't his day job, but he desperately wanted it to be throughout our time together.

I was walking past this shop, and before my brain could comprehend what my other body parts were doing, my feet had stomped in and my fingers found themselves rifling through the alphabetised CDs, specifically the section starting with the letter of Bruno's last name. It didn't take long before I saw it. Him. He was compact in any case, but here, in front of me, was the disc version of him. Wow. He'd actually made a record, or an extended play, to be precise. Bruno wasn't a man of many words, so it made sense that he didn't have enough for an album. Nonetheless, I was compelled to hear what he did have to say. My curiosity unconsciously crossed the fine line into crazy, and I bought the CD.

There was a McDonald's nearby, so I took myself there after leaving the record shop. Over French fries and a strawberry milkshake, I read through the glossy booklet that was tucked into the jewel case of Bruno's CD. He had always fancied himself as Bruno Mars. But this? This was more Mars Bar. My God, the lyrics of those six songs were so sickly sweet that I was surprised my teeth didn't rot and fall out as I mouthed them to myself – and also that my digestive system could survive that amount of cheesiness. It was as though that five-cheese risotto from our first date had been doused in treacle. I waded through the song words and eventually made it to the back page: the acknowledgements. Here I found lots of words of thanks, seemingly to everyone he'd ever met, whether they'd helped with the record or not. I recognised the names of some of his friends, and his hairdresser. Then he thanked his wife. Yes, his wife. I'd found out that he'd married a little while ago because my friend Gemma is a Facebook stalking genius and showed me photos. I noted that Bruno's wife had a nose as straight as a neck, what's known as a 'Greek nose' – he must have been trying to repeat something. After that, there was a final mention. One small sentence for one small person: 'Dedicated to my unborn daughter.'

There they were: five words that told me who Bruno was.

They were followed by five more words: 'Can't wait to meet you.'

I took a big gulp of my milkshake straight from the cup. Oh my God. Bruno has a baby on the way? In the womb of some other woman? Or maybe his child is now here, alive, on this earth? I looked over my shoulder and surveyed the entire restaurant from the corner where I was sitting, as though I expected to see Bruno with a baby in a buggy walk in at exactly that moment. I took another swig of my shake. Then I downed it, wishing it was hard liquor that would knock me out cold. All my cold milkshake did was give me brain freeze and a pink milk moustache. The child at the next table started pointing and giggling at me. But I didn't care; at least it disguised my top lip, which had started to do this weird wibble-wobble thing. My hands were trembling too. The only part of me that was stable were my eyes, which kept staring at the words in front of me.

My unborn daughter.

Can't wait to meet you.

Remember I told you in Chapter 3 that the Strange Situation happens with a child at around one year old? Well, we were one year on and this was a very strange situation: Bruno had a child. This was the real goodbye. No reunion. Bruno was now a husband and a father. It felt so Fast, and I was now starting to feel Furious. Fucking

Furious. My French fry fingers had smeared grease and salt all over the booklet but that wasn't enough to cover up those words, so I ripped it up. Then I released the disc from the case, cracked it into quarters and put the broken pieces in my cup, hoping they would drown in the dregs of my milkshake.

I don't remember much about the rest of that day, except for crying a lot. And making mashed potatoes, which really should have been called bashed and battered potatoes. I Kartoffelstampfed to high hell. To say I was heavy-handed would be an understatement. The olive oil splished and splashed everywhere, including on me, which I actually didn't mind because it felt like some kind of baptism; at that moment, in my mashed potato pit of despair, I wanted to be born again. That night, those potatoes didn't need any salt because my tears seasoned them. And because life had now given me this great big lemon, I didn't add any to my mash. A year ago, this very potato masher was in a box labelled 'Kitchen Stuff', as we packed up and moved out of our flat. Now Bruno was in some other kitchen using a mini food processor to purée veg and sterilising baby bottles for a baby he now wanted and couldn't wait to meet. Unlike our baby. My God. It felt like he had completely stampfed all over my heart. Again.

I couldn't even find comfort in the mashed potatoes that night. Or in food, or cooking, for quite some time after. I had, unexpectedly, tripped up on my grief, like a needle on a scratched record. If Bowlby and Parkes had seen me, they would have said this was bereavement, which is much more than grief alone. Bereavement faces us with major life changes. The Bruno-baby news was certainly that. Bereavement is also sometimes associated with shame, which I found in my thoughts and also when I looked in the mirror; staring back at me was a shame-faced consciousness that I wasn't good enough. I didn't have the right womb or the right nose or whatever would have been necessary for a family life with Bruno. For a good while, the white in my own fried egg model of grief shrunk away like a scared ghost, as I found out first-hand how complicated grief can be. Grief says, 'Hello, I'm here' when you least expect it. In fact, that's the only expectation you can have of grief. It also doesn't look like what you think it's going to look like, or do what you think it's going to do.

This is why I found myself disagreeing with Nora Ephron about something other than mashed potatoes: in her film *Julie and Julia* (which is inspired by Julia Child's life and recipes), the character of Julie makes a chocolate cream pie after a difficult day and says that when nothing is sure, you can absolutely know that if you add egg yolks to chocolate and sugar and milk, it will get thick. But what if you turn up the heat too much? Your chocolate custard will end up overcooked, with nasty eggy taste. Have you ever tried to whip egg whites in a bowl with even the faintest smear of grease? They'll whip, but they'll collapse faster than a chocolate teapot.

There is no such thing as a sure thing when it comes to eggs. Or grief. And sometimes eggs can curdle your grief. That's what happened to my patient Jojo.

***

'It's a bit weird to know someone's death day but not their birthday,' Jojo said, as she turned her head to look out the window.

Jojo had hardly looked at me during our session.

As we sat together, a pregnant silence hung in the room. Outside, the sky clouded over and daylight excluded itself, but Jojo continued looking for it out of the window. She shuffled in her chair and crossed her long legs, which were covered in black cobwebbed tights that grew out of her platform boots. They were usual features of Jojo's goth style, along with her poker-straight black hair and glossy, smoky-shadowed eyelids, which looked like large beetle husks. Everything looked blacker against her milky-white skin. Black was her colour. I had never seen Jojo wear white.

I stayed out of the space to let Jojo find her feelings. Or at least, words other than 'weird'. After all, weird is a judgement. I think I knew what she was judging herself for.

Jojo turned her head so her face was now back in the room with me. She hadn't found any feelings, but she had found a memory she wanted to share.

'Did I ever tell you that I made a cake, on the day she would have been a year old? Weird, huh?' said Jojo. 'I didn't plan to. I was in Waitrose one day and I saw a recipe card for this cake. It was an Easter cake, so cute and cheerful, with little mini eggs on top. I just wanted to make it. So I bought all the ingredients there and then. Everything: the sultanas, the currants, the glacé cherries, the marzipan and the chocolate eggs to decorate. I had everything ready, and I waited until the exact date to bake it. If anyone knew, they would think I was so weird. It's not exactly socially acceptable to make a birthday cake for someone who was never born.'

Jojo had been pregnant two years before she came to see me. In our first session, when I asked what brought her to therapy, Jojo said: 'Well, I was pregnant.' Her eyes had searched the room as if she was looking for something, then they stopped and looked down at her empty lap. There was no baby. The pregnancy had, in her words, ended with Jojo knowing her baby's 'death day': she'd had an abortion. It had happened when Jojo was twenty-one years old and in her final year at university. She and her then-boyfriend Ben 'weren't really serious' and the pregnancy was unplanned. Jojo's mother was horrified that a baby would ruin Jojo's career and that she would be throwing away an opportunity to do her PhD, which was in the pipeline for when she finished her degree. Jojo's mother was also worried about the judgement Jojo would face, having a baby out of wedlock. She told Jojo to have an abortion before it was too late, then Jojo could 'just move on'. Ben was also clear he didn't want the baby. Jojo had tried to explain to Ben how

she felt, and her doubt about whether it was the right deci-
sion, but his response was the sister comment to 'just move
on': 'you're overthinking it'. When Jojo said this, I found
myself feeling angry on her behalf. I've never understood
exactly what 'overthinking' is. Is there a 'just right' amount
of thinking? Of course there isn't. Neither Ben nor Jojo's
mother had the authority to decide the absolutes of how
much thought was allowed, or what she should do. Not
once had anyone asked Jojo what she wanted. She'd had
abandonment instead of support. Given what Jojo had
experienced from her loved ones, it made sense that she
had buried her feelings. A few days after finding out she
was pregnant, she made an appointment to have an abortion. She said she wanted it 'over and done with quickly'.

Jojo had gone on her own to have the abortion. She had
few words to describe the process, which, in some ways,
said it all: 'In. Pills. Out. Home. Pessaries. Gone.' But she
did go into detail about one part of the day. 'In the waiting room, I noticed a mother and a daughter sitting there.
They had a really big Pret A Manger bag with them – it
looked like they were making a day of it. I wondered if
they were planning to go to the park afterwards to picnic
with the rest of the food. The daughter ate her granola
yoghurt pot as she sat cross-legged on her chair, and the
mother put her hand on her knee. She didn't take it away.
The daughter looked young. She had baby-pink high tops
on. I had a similar pair when I was sixteen.'

Buried beneath Jojo's grief for the baby she never had was her grief for the mother she never had. I later learned that she had spent a lot of her life away from her mother, having boarded at school since she was eleven years old. Jojo had been terribly homesick during her school years. She said that one of the hardest things was watching the other girls receive weekly letters and care packages with sweets from their parents, and also birthday cakes. Jojo said, 'school was like the cake and sugar house in Hansel and Gretel'. But there was no trail of crumbs or cakes or letters to connect Jojo to home. Jojo's mother never sent her anything, not even on her birthday.

Jojo had found her anger after the abortion, and straight away she split up with both Ben and her family. She was still estranged and isolated when we started working together. Jojo spent most of her time doing her PhD, which was on nineteenth-century literature. Her dream, however, was to be a novelist, and she had recently started writing her first book. By writing about other people's lives, I wondered whether Jojo was trying to find words for her own.

So Jojo was a writer, not a baker. In our session that day, I noticed that she had gone on to change the subject, leaving the story about the cake half-baked. I was curious, so I asked her what happened.

'What? The would-be birthday cake? Nothing. The mix split into lumps. Couldn't be rescued. So I poured it down the sink. Washed it away,' Jojo said.

It was the shortest food story in the world. Birthday cake: no birth, never baked.

I found myself thinking about what had gone wrong with the cake Jojo tried to make to commemorate her baby: the batter had curdled. That tends to happen if you beat the eggs too fast into the butter and sugar. I wondered about Jojo's patience beyond baking. It seemed that Jojo expected the therapy, and her grief, to be quicker than it was. In the few months we had been working together, there was one question she'd asked me several times: 'What should I do to get over my grief?' To me, her question felt like another way of saying, 'I want to get rid of my grief'. Today, there we were talking about cake, when really, we were talking about the slow pain of grief that Jojo just couldn't wash away, no matter how much she wanted to.

Parkes told me there is an important difference between grief before and after loss. He said with grief that follows loss, we learn to live without our loved one. But grief before loss leads to more preoccupation with the other person; in other words, greater attachment. This was Jojo. In the days leading up to her abortion, Jojo had become more and more attached to her baby. She had decided that the baby was a girl. She had calculated her own due date. She'd found a week-by-week 'How big is my baby?' guide on Netmums, which, just before the date of her appointment, said her baby was about the size of a cake sprinkle. She'd got herself a Baby on Board badge to wear on the bus. She had 'taken the baby for coffee' and ordered a babyccino; she'd kept the little cup and straw. Her mind was filled with her baby. Filled with love. I could empathise. All this love for someone who would never love you back; it was the ultimate unrequited love. It was clear to me how much Jojo wanted to hold on to her baby. But the most heartbreaking part of the story was when she tried to – literally. Just after Jojo had passed the baby, she knelt at the toilet, plunged her hands into the bloodied bowl and scurried around, trying to find the foetus. Now, whenever I hear people talk about 'searching' in the phases of grief, this image of Jojo immediately comes to my mind. I think it always will. Some things never leave you.

***

Whenever I hear the term 'love letter', I think of a time with Jojo some months after we spoke about the would-be birthday cake. It was a spring day, and towards the end of our session, Jojo opened her studded black leather backpack and took out a single sheet of folded paper. She said that now, on what would have been a second birthday, she wanted to give her baby, and her grief, something. This time she hadn't baked a cake. She had written a letter.

'Would you mind if I read it to you?' Jojo asked.

'I'd be privileged to hear it,' I said.

Jojo unfolded the letter. It started to shake ever so gently in the long, spindly fingers of her hands. My mind flashed forwards, or possibly backwards, or perhaps to a place not bound by time – and I pictured Jojo doing the most perfect

rendition of the Incy Wincy Spider with those same fingers. As she started to read to me, her voice was warm and
maternal. It was the voice of story time, and Jojo in the
book corner with her baby.

17 March 2017

My little one,
Today is your birthday. Happy birthday baby! But
you're not a baby anymore. Today you are two. There
is something wonderful about you being born on this
day of the year, St Patrick's Day. It makes me smile
because I know you would have been mischievous and
magical, just like a little leprechaun. And you would
have stolen my heart away. Maybe this is just like the
folktale? Maybe I'm the human that captured you?
Maybe I set you free, and you might grant me three
wishes? Maybe that's too much to ask of you. I really
have no right given what I did.

I wanted to write you this letter because there is
something I need to say: I wish I had changed my
mind before that fateful day. It was weird how it felt
like an ordinary weekday. There were people everywhere, going about their busy business, stopping for
their cappuccinos and lattes then going back out,
walking and running up and down the streets. As all
those people passed by me, they had no idea. I left
home with you and came back without you. People

were still crawling all over the streets, but I imagine they were going home by that time.

You had your little home inside me and I made you homeless. The cramps felt like you were using your tiny fists to say, 'Hello, I'm here.' Like you were fighting for your life. I am so sorry I never did that for you. I wish I had. I wish I hadn't listened to them. I made the wrong choice. I don't think I will ever forgive myself, but I hope that you might forgive me.

I can't believe I was nearly your mummy. Me, *your* mummy.

Jojo stopped reading.

'Can I say "mummy"? Is that allowed?' she said, as though she was a child who'd been caught with her hand in the cookie jar. Her eyes looked helplessly up into mine. As I gazed back at Jojo, I could see that her heart wasn't young and fresh and whole anymore: it was bruised and broken, and it was still breaking right there in front of me. I gave up trying to find the right thing to say or do, and I answered not as a psychotherapist, but as a woman who had nearly been a mummy too.

'Yes. Yes, it is,' I said, not wanting to take my eyes off her, not even for a second.

Jojo put the letter down on the coffee table between us.

'I really wanted my ba—,' She started to sob, unable to make it to the end of 'baby'. Her tears overflowed. My heart went out to her. At that moment, all I could do was show

Jojo that I got it. Because I did. I knew that pain. As her tears fell fast on her hands, I gave her two words to hold.

'I know,' I said, hoping this would show Jojo that I understood her and that she was visible to me. I could see her handwritten feelings too, from where I was sitting. The last words of her letter were:

I wish I had you.

Love,
Mummy

Jojo had given her sorrow words. And the truth, both spoken and written, had started to set her free.

***

When my grief became complicated after finding out about Bruno and his baby, I also found myself asking my Delia the same question that Jojo had asked me: 'What should I do to get over it?' When I said it, there in our session that day, I wasn't even sure what I meant by 'it'. My relationship with Bruno himself? Or the fact that he now had a family? But Delia knew. She knew I was talking about my baby. Somehow, she let me know that, because then I started to cry. We had silence for a minute, as I let out my tears and as Delia let in my words. I could see through my misty eyes that she was really thinking about what I had asked her. She cocked her head to the side, looked straight at me and repeated my question, empha- sising one particular word with her voice: '*What* should you do to get over it?' Then she replaced that word and asked me a different question: '*Why* should you get over it? Sometimes in life we are possessed by death. No mat- ter what, you will never find a substitute. Whatever might fill the gap will always be something else. And actually, this is the way it should be with love we do not wish to relinquish.'

I don't know if Delia was aware that she had perfectly mixed and mingled the words of Bowlby, Freud, T. S. Eliot and Nora Ephron in her answer. But what I did know is that I would remember her words forever.

There are times in therapy when people want permission to get over things. But what we might need even more is permission not to get over it. The aim of therapy, always, is to create choice and freedom. With attachment the- ory, Bowlby challenged the assumption that a 'normal' or 'healthy' person can, and should, get over a loss, not just quickly but completely. Parkes also said something very similar to me at our lunch that day. He said that a bereaved person might find another partner or have another baby, but people are not interchangeable or replaceable. Every indi- vidual is unique, so each person we love is priceless. That's why an attachment bond is not easily detachable. Some even say it can never really be broken. Jojo didn't have to detach; she didn't have to relinquish her love if she didn't want to. There was no reason why she should get over the loss of her baby. When we ended our work many years later, Jojo told me that was the best thing I ever said to her.

***

At the start of this chapter, I told you a story about a cake that didn't happen. If you remember, at the beginning of this book I also told you about another time and place where food never happened. That story was about a man who closed the door on food when he was creating the most significant theory about love and relationships. Why did he do that? Because he'd been rejected by his peers. Bowlby may have been the father of attachment theory, but he was human and, like any other human being, he brought who he was — attachment wounds and all — into his work. Sometimes there are things you just can't leave at the door.

As for Ainsworth, while the loss of her baby never left her, it defined her work within attachment theory. Ainsworth's longing for motherhood became her research gift. She felt it gave her a kind of insight that she could use to understand mother–infant interactions. It's true; she had an extraordinary ability to see and feel the world through a baby's eyes. Her research was her reorganisation, and her work allowed her to grow around her grief in a special way. I know that being a therapist has helped me to do the same; I guess it's true what the psychoanalyst Carl Jung said about therapists being 'wounded healers'.

If you have been hurt in a relationship, whether a rejection or a separation or a loss, then you need to be healed in a relationship. That's the heart of how therapy works, but that healing can happen in other relationships too. Many years after her miscarriage, Ainsworth talked about her disappointment fading and being replaced with something else good: her academic family of students, whose lives were important to her. My patients mean the same to me. I may not have my baby, but now, because of my patients, I have something else good in every day. Maybe we did become mothers, after all.

In our last session, Jojo gave me two envelopes. Inside one was a thank-you card. Inside the other was the letter she had written to her 'little one'. She said she wanted me to have it. Perhaps she wanted to leave a piece of herself with me; and she did, in so many ways. The work, our work, was precious to me. Jojo recently got in touch to ask me something and in that conversation over email, I told her I was writing this book. She said that, if I wanted to, I could share her letter and her experience. Jojo expressed her hope that other people would be helped by her story and find comfort in what she had written. This is why you have seen and heard her words in this chapter. I am so grateful to Jojo for her brave generosity.

Jojo was my first baby-bereaved patient, so all of me – baby wounds and all – inevitably entered the room when we worked together. Her story has been significant for my own bereavement, and healing. So much so that one day I found myself wondering what birthday cake I might have made for my baby. I didn't make a cake. Instead, inspired by Jojo, I wrote a letter about it. It wasn't a sure thing, I just put one word after the other. I tried to give my sorrow words about cake, and this is where it took me:

Dear baby,

Hello.

Is that a good word to start with? They say hello is the moment when you 'have' a person, but I'm not sure about that. I can say hello to you, and I can introduce myself to you. But it won't change the fact that I don't have you. I cannot hold you. I don't know what that feels like.

There is so much I don't know about you. I don't know when your birthday would have been. I don't know what kind of cake you would have liked. But I know I would have made you a birthday cake each and every year. Today, all these cake thoughts were going round and round in my mind, like a merry-go-round. A funfetti cake bursting with rainbow sprinkles. An angel food cake, fluffier and lighter than a cloud. A really rich chocolate fudge cake. A homemade Colin the Caterpillar, which you would have said 'Mine!' to and gobbled up excitedly. They do say children love chocolate. But I don't have that photo of you with cocoa smudges around your little mouth. I do have a picture of you though, inside my mind. You have wild curls with all of autumn's colours. A round face with a sweetie button nose. A priceless smile. I have always been someone who is so alive to flaws, mostly my own. But you are perfect. That I know.

When I found out you were on the way, I had this feeling I have never had before. I felt full, like I would never hunger again. I was surprised and excited and, most of all, grateful. But that feeling scared me. You can't be grateful unless you want something. Or someone. I knew then how much I wanted you. I said hello to you.

The last day that I had you never leaves me. In the morning, I remember walking down the stairwell at the flat, the echoes of the grey, cold concrete steps. The wind was gentle but it didn't whisper; it sounded like it was wailing, like it was trying to tell me that something horrible was going to happen. I feel like I should've known. But I just didn't know. I didn't know we were saying goodbye. I didn't know you were leaving. Then it was too late. You were gone by the time dinner was over. I didn't get to say goodbye to you the way I wanted to.

I have imagined our home. Our kitchen. The table we would have eaten at, lived around and read 'Once upon a time' stories at. Perhaps you would have loved ghost stories. I liked *Funny Bones* when I was little; I wonder if you would have too. I know I would have loved you to your bones. I already did. Sometimes I feel so sad about not being able to have you; the feeling blows through me like a wild wind through a haunted house. But maybe that's what grief is – love that haunts you.

Sometimes, when I could see nothing else but black darkness, I have wished I hadn't said hello to you, because then I wouldn't have had to say goodbye.

But I want you to know that I would say it all over again, no matter what. You were worth it. I know that to the moon and back.

Love,
Mummy

Chapter 16

Post-Heartburn

Can you heal a broken bond with food?

Primo: the first course may be pasta, served sauced or in broth,
or it can be a risotto, or a soup.
Secondo: the second course is usually a development of the
theme established by the first, though sometimes the reverse
may also be true. If you are going to start with tagliatelle alla
bolognese (home-made noodles with meat sauce), you might
want to give your palate some relief by following with a simple
roast of veal or chicken.

Marcella Hazan, The Essentials of Classic Italian Cooking

It's one year later, and Rachele has remained in therapy
with me. She is still married to Marco, but they are not living together. Shortly after that session I told you about,
Rachele informed Marco that she wanted some space, and
she asked him to move out. Marco is now renting a small
studio flat nearby. This has given Rachele's heart some
relief. And Marco's palate.

Today, in our session, as I look at Rachele, I find myself
thinking about something my Delia once said: 'Sorrow

concealed is like an oven stopped: it burns the heart to cinders where it is.' Rachele is still striking, but her face is more furrowed now, which gives away her stricken heart. She hasn't concealed her sorrow, so her heart is not completely burned. But it is broken because there has been a loss.

After the chilli, Rachele went on to cake – metaphorically. She said about Marco: 'He can't eat his cake, shit it out and still have it.'

She is right. That's generally what affairs are about. Metaphorically.

Marco has told Rachele the affair(s) has/have stopped. He says it was just sex. Perhaps that was part of it, but it's never as simple as that. There are always feelings to explore, and this is something Rachele has discovered for herself. Over the last year her anger has simmered down, but the emotions hiding underneath are more complicated than she anticipated. The thing is, betrayal, hate and hurt don't cancel out love. It's holding these mixed feelings all at the same time that will allow Rachele to move on – and to forgive, if that's what she wants to do. Rachele's defences have cooled down too, which tends to happen as therapy goes on. She believes less in denial now: her experience has shown her that what you don't know can hurt you (and, as we've seen, what you don't know is in the ragù can hurt you even more).

None of this process has been a piece of cake for Rachele. I can see when she struggles in our sessions: she makes a tight fist with one hand and holds it with the other, as she did that day when she told me about the ragù. She is doing this now in our session. I notice the skin on her hands is thinner, and her spider veins are visible in a way they weren't before. But as I'm looking at them, Rachele breaks our moment of silence.

'I'm still his wife,' she tells me. Rachele repeats this phrase more than I think she is aware of in our sessions. Today she has said it twice already. Food has always, and still is, a large part of this identity. In fact, food is entwined into Rachele's life as a wife — still. Because Rachele still cooks, and Marco comes over for dinner every night.

Yes, you read that correctly. Every night. Since he moved out.

While there has been loss, now there is separation during the day and reunion at night. It might seem bewildering that Rachele and Marco have carried on eating dinner together every night, and that this part of their relationship has stayed the same. After all, Marco has lied and cheated. But that's not enough to break their bond, or for them to detach from dinner time. I'm reminded of what Rachel says in *Heartburn*, about cooking becoming the easy way of saying I love you, and then the only way of saying it. I wonder if it is the same for Rachele. As we know, food is the first way of saying I love you. That's why it's easy — because it's familiar.

Is it Cook, Eat, Repeat? Or, Cook, Eat, Repetition Compulsion, as Freud would say. I wonder whether they are unconsciously repeating the old and familiar because it's the only way they can feel safe.

In our conversation, Rachele then does something very familiar: she criticises the tie Marco was wearing yesterday evening at dinner. As she does, she glares at my chenille cardigan. I wait for a negative comment about my fashion faux pas too. It doesn't arrive, and she quickly moves on to say something else about Marco. Why didn't I raise it? Perhaps that would have felt too close, the idea that she might have some feelings about me. Or at least, my cardigan. Maybe I am allowing Rachele to be in control, so she feels safe. Just like in the kitchen. If Rachele cooks, then she is in control of the food — and the story.

In our session, Rachele tells me a story from last night's dinner with Marco.

'He told me he never ever ate any other woman's home-cooked food,' she says. 'Never. Nothing. Not a spoonful. In all the time we are married. Only mine.' I see her eyes brighten as she says this.

So Marco has been faithful when it comes to food. And in their own way, maybe they are looking at the infidelity together, through food. Perhaps they are not repeating. Maybe they are remembering and working through.

Cook, Eat, Repair?

In therapy, and as part of her own reparation, Rachele is getting to know herself more deeply. We are getting to know her history, and joining up the dots from past to present. Some months ago, I suggested Rachele draw a timeline to show key events in her life. Her attachment history isn't good on paper; there is a lot of loss and abandonment. And Marco isn't the only person who has had an affair. Rachele's parents were unfaithful to each other, and since both led double lives with other partners, they were often out of the house until late at night, even when Rachele was a child. From as early as she could remember, Rachele had taken care of herself. I found out that Rachele's mother hadn't taught her personally how to make the ragù. As soon as Rachele was old enough to read, her mother had given Rachele her recipe notebook and Rachele had learned to cook by using that. She cooked every day, not only for herself, but also so that there was food for when her parents did eventually return home. For most of her childhood and her adolescence, Rachele ate alone at the table.

When Rachele told me this, she had a light-bulb moment. She realised that Marco hasn't abandoned her. He sits at the table and eats with her every evening. He has done so for thirty years. The table, for better or for worse, is their place of connection. In their relationship, food is fundamental. That's actually another thing my Delia said: 'Freud was right: everything boils down to sex and death. After that, there's not much left really. Except for food.' She immediately followed that up with Hippocrates: 'Remember: Let food be thy medicine and medicine be thy food.' It resonated with me, because it seems to be what Rachele and Marco are doing.

I notice that Rachele doesn't talk about sex much in our sessions. I wonder if she and Marco will figure out the sex part of their marriage. If they don't, at least they will be faithful in food.

As for death? Well, my Delia believes in food after death. She told me she once had a dinner party where she served a peach pie for dessert (she had tried to make a soufflé but burned the roux). That evening, everyone went on and on about how sensational this pie was, but Delia said she couldn't take credit because her mother made it. Then someone said, 'But your mother died ten years ago,' to which Delia replied, 'It was in the freezer.'

Only my Delia and Sara Lee could get away with that. And probably my mother too, for that matter.

Today, Rachele and I talk about the mothers in her life, including Marco's mother, who took Rachele under her wing when they met. As I listen, I am struck by how much of an attachment figure she has been to Rachele. When Rachele and Marco first got married, they lived with Marco's mother in Florence for a few years before moving to the UK. Rachele's mother-in-law is now in her eighties, and she is an artist as well as a keen cook. Rachele has learned many things from her. First and foremost: don't overdo the garlic.

'She says, "What garlic is to salad, insanity is to art". A little improves it a lot, but after that it overpowers everything else, so you shouldn't go crazy with it,' Rachele explains.

Rachele's mother-in-law believes in garlic as a healer and a protector, not only for the body, but for the spirit and the soul. She is passionate about garlic's power to ward off the evil eye (the *malocchio*). Rachele points to the pendant on a thin gold chain around her neck. It was the first birthday present her mother-in-law gave her. Rachele tells me that her mother-in-law's secret to a beautiful salad is to first rub the bowl with a cut clove of garlic, before dressing it with plenty of salt, a generous glug of olive oil and a little vinegar. Then, you must be very patient as you toss, so that each ingredient touches the bowl. Her mother-in-law does this for all her *insalata*, as well as her vegetables (her *contorni*), whether grilled, sautéed or boiled. Rachele says her mother-in-law doesn't own a recipe book – she's never heard of Marcella Hazan, Anna Del Conte or Pellegrino Artusi.

The first chapter of Artusi's book, *Science in the Kitchen and the Art of Eating Well*, is called 'The Story of a Book that Is a Bit Like the Story of Cinderella'. I wonder whether Rachele and Marco will live happily ever after. I just don't know. But it's not my job to know. It's my job to help Rachele know for herself. To discover what she believes, her own truth, and to make her own choices. Therapy doesn't offer quick fixes or guarantees. It's not a recipe accompanied by a bright, glossy photograph that says, 'Ta-da! This is what the finished you will look like!' What I do know is that Rachele and Marco need to go back to the beginning and build their relationship again. But this time more securely, with a solid foundation of trust. They need to share their thoughts and feelings instead of bottling them up and acting them out. They need to find a safe haven in each other. They need to be vulnerable. Rachele will need to let Marco into the shell.

This is what attachment theory calls earning security.

In the early days of attachment theory, Ainsworth said that food and attachment were 'entangled'. Nora Ephron once said something similar, which I quoted at the start of this book: 'when food and love become hopelessly tangled.' But from what I've seen over the years, I don't think it's ever hopeless when food and love tangle themselves together – it just shows we're human. Although, sadly there's no hope for the relationship at the end of *Heartburn*: Rachel throws a key lime pie at Mark and then leaves him. There have been no pie-ings in Rachele and Marco's relationship in the last year, so perhaps that's a hopeful sign, as well as the fact that neither of them is leaving the other behind at dinner time. Maybe what is most hopeful is that Rachele has kept coming to see me: therapy cannot exist without the presence of hope.

Our session comes to an end. The rain came down earlier, but now the sun has come out. As Rachele puts on her leather jacket, she tells me she is going to the butcher on her way home to pick up some meat for dinner tonight. I can't help myself: I'm curious. I ask her what she is cooking.

'Ossobuco in Bianco. Braised veal shanks. No tomatoes. The simple, classic one,' she says.

I smile at her. I imagine Rachele has made this dish hundreds of times. In life, and in the kitchen, things come around again. But nothing stays the same.

Except for the butcher. He is still useless.

As Rachele leaves, I tell her I am looking forward to seeing her next week.

* * *

Gently Garlicked Mashed Potatoes

Inspired by Rachele's mother-in-law. And not a knob of butter in sight.

Serves 2

500g potatoes (Cyprus potatoes, if you can get them; if not, any slightly yellow-fleshed waxy potato such as Desirée or other red-skinned potato)
¾ teaspoon salt
100ml extra virgin olive oil
1 garlic clove

Peel the potatoes, cut them into large chunks and place in a large saucepan with just enough cold water to cover them, along with ½ teaspoon of salt. Bring to the boil, lower the heat and cover the pan. Gently boil the potatoes for about 10–15 minutes, or until you can easily insert a knife through the potato chunk.

Drain the potatoes well and leave them in a colander over the pan to steam-dry for a few minutes. Mash them using a potato masher or by passing them through a potato ricer or a sieve.

Return the potatoes to the pan. Place the pan back on a low heat and add the olive oil and the rest of the salt. Slowly beat until combined and you have smooth, soft mash, then remove from the heat.

Cut the garlic clove in half and rub it around your serving bowl several times. Decant your mashed potatoes into the bowl. Stir gently a couple of times so that the mash mixes and mingles with the garlic.

I want to tell you a funny story about my Delia. You may have noticed that I dedicated this book to her. She means a lot to me. For many years now, she has been my backbone, and because of our work, I have been able to find more wishbones than I ever imagined. I guess what I'm saying is that she has been my secure base.

One day, fairly recently, I was in our session and I was being a bit 'woe-is-me-I-have-writer's-block', as I was struggling with the *Heartburn* chapter at the time. As part of that conversation, I was telling Delia all about Nora Ephron.

Delia nodded and said, 'Yes, yes. I've just ordered Nora Ephron's autobiography.'

Now at this point I hadn't said *Heartburn* to Delia, or said that I was thinking of giving a chapter that title, so I didn't know whether Delia meant *Heartburn*, because it's not exactly an autobiography. But I didn't tell Delia that, because she seemed quite excited, and unconsciously I probably didn't want to be one of those know-it-all patients. Delia normally reads Dostoevsky or T. S. Eliot, so I was pleased to hear that she was finally going to read something a little funnier.

But then Delia said that Amazon had taken her money, screwed up her order, found her order, tried to deliver her order, screwed that up and in the end told her it was out of print, which is a blatant lie.

Then I said: 'I wonder how you feel about that.'

And she said, 'Bastards!'

I realise that Delia is not the only person who has had that sort of experience with Amazon – that is not a strange situation at all. But it was the way she said 'Bastards!' with her mouth enthusiastically stretched wide open, like she was at the dentist or about to burst into a rendition of 'Baa, Baa, Black Sheep'.

I thought it was funny, in any case. I do think my Delia has quite the funny bone, but it was probably one of those times when you had to be there. It was 'ha ha' funny, but it was also 'aha' funny, in that it was a moment of synchronicity, as Jung would say. It was also a moment of playfulness, trust and connection. In other words, attachment.

In *Heartburn*, Rachel says to her therapist, Vera, who is married to a man named Niccolo, that she sometimes wishes they would get a divorce, because their marriage is very hard on the rest of the therapy group. I don't feel that way. Well, my Delia isn't married. She and her partner Nigel 'haven't got around to it yet'. They have been together for nearly fifty years.

I don't even know why I was explaining to Delia who Nora Ephron was. There's no way she could not know because Nigel is a screenwriter, and he even did a stint in Hollywood early on in his career. I have no idea what Nigel looks like. I picture him grey and bearded with blue eyes, like the chef Marcus Wareing. I am pretty sure Nigel does most of the cooking in their household. Maybe he makes a legendary custard tart, just like the one Marcus Wareing made for the Queen's eightieth birthday banquet. I also imagine Nigel is charming and sophisticated and devoted. Delia told me that just before they began courting, Nigel received a romantic proposition from a starlet who is now a famous actress, but he turned her down because he knew in his heart Delia was the one. When Delia said that, the corners of her mouth curled upwards into a little smile. It was very sweet to see her act a tad teenagery. I love that my Delia has love in her life.

It gives me hope.

Lately, I have felt hopeful.

I wonder if it's because I have started dating someone.

I think I quite like him.

Delia seems to think so too, because I have been talking about him in therapy. A lot. The other day, she suggested I pop by his house to see him ('Tell him you were just passing').

Anyway, it's too early to say anything more. But what I will say is that we have been out for a burger date and he picked up his big burger – two thick beef patties bulging out of a sesame seed bun — with both hands, and he ate it with gusto. With each bite, the meaty juices dribbled down into his beard. At that moment, I could see myself becoming quite attached to him.

I don't know where it's going.

But it isn't the worst way to begin.

RECIPE INDEX

A

Apple pie, 13
Avgolemoni, 30

C

Cheese and Onion Crisp-Chips, 213

E

Egg in a Hole, 245

F

Fairy Cakes, 91

G

Gently Garlicked Mashed
    Potatoes, 275
Greek Baked Beans, 128

K

Kataifi Nests, 114

L

Lemon Mahalebi Tart, 176

M

Macaronia Tou
    Fournou, 232

O

Ouzo Calamari, 47

S

Spaghetti with Tomato
    Sauce, 196

T

Tea-ramisu, 66
Tyrokafteri Tagliatelle, 157

W

Watermelon Tzatziki, 145

AUTHOR'S NOTE

In writing this book, it is important to say that in one respect I have been decidedly unlike Nora Ephron: everything has been thickly disguised. What you have read is drawn from stories I have heard over the years, but I have taken care to protect my patients' confidentiality and made many changes accordingly; I have altered all identifying details, and mixed, mingled and entwined narratives for anonymity. You may have noticed I use the word 'patient' rather than 'client' to refer to people in therapy. My choice of terminology takes heed from John Bowlby himself, but is also because of the original meaning of 'patient' as 'the one who suffers', which is, after all, why people tend to come to therapy. And, as Rachele's mother-in-law says: you must be patient. In the kitchen, and in therapy.

ACKNOWLEDGEMENTS

The food writer Margaret Visser once said, 'food is never just something to eat'. Similarly, a book isn't just something to write: it has given me connections with people I never thought possible. Thank you to my amazing agents, Jonny Geller, Viola Hayden and Ciara Finan: the dream team. I am so proud to be a part of Curtis Brown. Since the start of this journey at Curtis Brown Creative, I have felt taken care of, and I am grateful to Ali Shaw, Laura Barnett and my fellow Jackalopes for giving me so much thoughtful feedback on my writing along the way. My heartfelt thanks go to Jennifer Kerslake: she sent an email that changed my life and I will be forever indebted to her for that. A big thank you to everyone at Bloomsbury for making me feel so welcome. In that very first email, my editor Katy Follain, said that she 'LOVED' the proposal for *The Kitchen Shrink*. Well, I have LOVED working with her! Thank you Katy for *everything*, most of all for understanding how much of a baby this book has been to me. To my managing editors, Lauren Whybrow and Faye Robinson, and my copyeditor Laura Gladwin, thank you for your brilliance, diligence and guidance.

I have several attachment figures whom I would like to thank for their support. My incredible book coach, Beth Miller: you didn't just help me 'get near it', you helped me actually *get it* – I couldn't have written this book without you (and if I had, it would have much less rhythm and the word 'pineapples' would be in it). Catherine Jacobs: you are such a special friend to me and solid gold support in every single way. Claire and Mark Anderson: huge thanks for simple dinners and for regulating my complicated feelings. Angela Clow and Chantal Gautier: together you are my Beaufort Bar Belles and individually you have each given me a great deal of TLC. Catherine Loveday: to me you will always be Catherine Lovely. Gemma Reynolds: thank you for being there and for always wanting to know what I've had for dinner.

Thank you to each and every one of my patients, whose stories have found their way into my heart and my kitchen. I am so grateful to Rory Elliott, my extraordinary supervisor, who has helped me to grow as a therapist. Thanks to my wonderful colleagues at all of my professional homes: Middlesex University, the University of Westminster and the Bowlby Centre, especially Linda Cundy for taking me from cradle to kitchen in the first place.

Thank you to my family. Johnny, you are the best brother: all of those onions you ate really did make you big and strong and Great. Dad: I love your rendition of 'Mary Had a Little Lamb' and I love that because of you I have learned to never mind the bollocks. Mum: thank you for love, patience and kindness that is expressed in Mum Food and beyond. But please, for the love of God, stop bringing me poussins – my freezer is full of them.

A NOTE ON THE AUTHOR

Andrea Oskis is a psychologist, food writer and professional cook. She is interested in two of the things that are essential for human survival: relationships and food. Her academic expertise is human relationships – how we love and connect with each other – and she has researched, taught and written about this for more than twenty years. Andrea's food writing has been published in *Vittles*, *Pit Magazine* and *Gastronomica*, *The Journal for Food Studies*. She is a member of the Guild of Food Writers. In 2022, Andrea was shortlisted for Moniack Mhor's Emerging Writer of the Year and a Guild of Food Writers Award. In 2023, she won the M.F.K. Fisher Last House Writing Contest. The following year, Andrea was made a Fellow of the British Psychological Society.

A NOTE ON THE TYPE

The text of this book is set in Fournier. Fournier is derived from the romain du roi, which was created towards the end of the seventeenth century from designs made by a committee of the Académie of Sciences for the exclusive use of the Imprimerie Royale. The original Fournier types were cut by the famous Paris founder Pierre Simon Fournier in about 1742. These types were some of the most influential designs of the eighteenth century and are counted among the earliest examples of the 'transitional' style of typeface. This Monotype version dates from 1924. Fournier is a light, clear face whose distinctive features are capital letters that are quite tall and bold in relation to the lower-case letters, and *decorative italics, which show the influence of the calligraphy of Fournier's time.*